FAITHFUL

Introduction by **AMY GRANT**

AMANDA BIBLE WILLIAMS   RAECHEL MYERS

ANN VOSKAMP   RUTH CHOU SIMONS

GINNY OWENS   SALLY LLOYD-JONES

KELLY MINTER   SARAH MACINTOSH

KELLY NEEDHAM   SAVANNAH LOCKE

LISA HARPER   TRILLIA NEWBELL

FAITHFUL

Published by David C Cook
4050 Lee Vance Drive
Colorado Springs, CO 80918 U.S.A.

Integrity Music Limited, a Division of David C Cook
Brighton, East Sussex BN1 2RE, England

The graphic circle C logo is a registered trademark of David C Cook.
Faithful is a trademark of Compassion International, Inc., and used herein under license.

The website addresses recommended throughout this book are offered as a resource to you. These websites are not intended in any way to be or imply an endorsement on the part of David C Cook, nor do we vouch for their content.

Details in some stories have been changed to protect the identities of the persons involved.

Library of Congress Control Number 202094941
ISBN 978-0-8307-8173-7
eISBN 978-0-8307-8174-4

© 2021 David C Cook

Cover and Interior Design: Morgan Brewer and Studio Antheia Team
Primary Photographer: Joy Prouty

First Edition 2021

1 2 3 4 5 6 7 8 9 10

011321

Enter his gates with thanksgiving
and his courts with praise;
give thanks to him and praise his name.
For the LORD is good
and his love endures forever;
his faithfulness continues through all generations.

PSALM 100:4–5

The Art House, Nashville

THE FAITHFUL PROJECT

was created to unite the voices of authors, artists, and songwriters in telling the story of God's faithfulness, particularly toward women in the Bible, to women of today who seek assurance of His continued faithfulness toward them.

Album · Book · Podcast · Events

@THEFAITHFULPROJECT

WWW.FAITHFULPROJECT.COM

This book is dedicated to the women
in our lives: *past, present, and future ...*

Vivian Rankins   Phyllis Chipp   Jacquelyn M. Reddick-Jones   Iris
Reddick Rose Archer Jasmine Daniel Wynde Jones-Reddick Robin
Shyne-Briggs   Millie Long   Sarah Besenius   Corrina Gill   Jenny
Gill Van Valkenburg   Kathy Harrell   Mimi Verner   Carol Nuismer
Patricia Brown Angel   Theresa Harper Bruno   Melissa Price Harper
Bee Hogue   Nell Bannister   Debbie Bannister   Carly Bannister
Emmylou Holcomb Valerie Lloyd-Jones Siân Prentice Juliet Blight
Ellie Blight   Emily Prentice   Olivia Prentice   Gwynn Wills   Gloria
Dudney   Rene Jordan   Beth Goins   Anne Templeton   Sarah Jordan
Betty Ann Kroger   Danielle Kroger   Nancy Sannicandro   Marianne
Harrington Colleen Lampa   Joanna Lampa   Christy Lampa   Denise
Leonhardt   Toni Finsterwald   Corinna Girard   Asia Ali   Carter
Webb   Betty McCracken   Jennifer Patterson   Scarlett MacIntosh
Laurie Meeker   Rachel Meeker   Deedee   Nanny   Kay Minter   Megan
Minter   Katie Gates   Megen Minter   Hazel Myers   Evie Grace Myers
Rebecca Faires   Beatrice Faires   Susan Bumpus   Beverly Myers   Mary

those whose stories have, are, and will shape our own.

Adams Abby Patton Lively Needham Sophia Needham Armelia Reed Jean Newbell Sydney Newbell Barbara Hodge Tennion Reed Alicia McCleary Elizabeth McCleary Susan Hill Elliana Nockels Annie Rose Nockels Margie Owens Emily Dippel Carol Lloyd Ginger Ostenson Jennifer Ostenson Elizabeth Ray Nancy Ray Samantha Ray Linda Simons Julia Chou Gina Adams Kenzie Watson Camille Davis Sarah Alexander Linda Morton Gerry Voskamp Hope Voskamp Shalom Voskamp Shiloh Voskamp Sofia Colene Wells Olivia Rowan Wells Sherrie Rogers Brenda Bible Etta Williams Susan Williams Jennifer Bible Trisha Williams Susan Ellis Ashley Elorza Emily Chadwell Christy Nockels Heather McCollum Rylie McCollum Deborah McCollum Dorothy McCollum Pauline Lewis Alison Osenga Donna Osenga Carolyn Shipley Ella Osenga Sadie Osenga Charlotte Osenga Penny Burrows Shelley Verdes Meghan McPherson Jillian McPherson Elizabeth Deal Madonna Burrows Everley Marie Scott Kelsey Harp Kathy Orr

TABLE of CONTENTS

Each chapter mirrors songs on the companion album
Faithful: Go and Speak.

Introduction
AMY GRANT   *12*

RAHAB

God's Faithfulness in Our Professions / *Amanda Bible Williams*   *16*

RUTH

God's Faithfulness in Our Disillusion / *Kelly Minter*   *30*

JEHOSHEBA

God's Faithfulness in Obscurity / *Kelly Needham*   *46*

THE BENT WOMAN

God's Faithfulness in Our Pain and Disappointment / *Lisa Harper*   *62*

LEAH

God's Faithfulness in Rejection / *Ruth Chou Simons*   *80*

EVE

The Story of Eve / *Sally Lloyd-Jones*   *92*

MARY MAGDALENE

God's Faithfulness in Release / *Savannah Locke*   *108*

NAOMI

God's Faithfulness in Tragedy / *Trillia Newbell*   *122*

ESTHER

God's Faithfulness to Us Nobodies / *Raechel Myers*   *134*

MIRIAM

God's Faithfulness in the Middle of the Story / *Ann Voskamp*   *150*

HANNAH

God's Faithfulness When Life Feels Unfair / *Ginny Owens*   *164*

REFLECTIONS

Sarah Macintosh   182

THE STORY OF FAITHFUL   196

ACKNOWLEDGMENTS   202

NOTES   204

L to R: Sandra McCracken, Trillia Newbell, Kelly Minter, Sarah Macintosh, Leslie Jordan, Amanda Bible Williams, Sally Lloyd-Jones
Backs facing L to R: Raechel Meyers, Ruth Chou Simons

Photo by Cameron Powell

Faithful

Introduction

BY AMY GRANT

In the fall of 2019 I was invited to a two-day creative workshop.

The attendees would be women: songwriters, poets, speakers, and storytellers.

The purpose: to build community with each other while considering the unique experiences of women mentioned in the Bible.

The goal: to create conversation, songs and essays inspired by these women from the past, and possibly see our present lives as each being a part of God's continuing epic story of redemption and love ... which, by the way, is quite a messy story.

If it is true that we are surrounded by a great cloud of unseen witnesses, I imagine several of our female ancestors elbowing their way to the front of the circle shouting, "Girls, you don't know the half of it! But we tried."

Together we read the scant accounts of each woman's situation, acknowledging historical place and time, imagining all the unaccounted-for details that filled their lives.

We imagined the opportunity and the oppression.

With empathy and compassion we held these women with our creative attention ... in silence, in conversation, over lunch and through dinner, until their stories became our stories, until their voices became our voices.

Isn't that the kind of listening that changes each of us? To listen well enough and long enough to another's life song until we can sing it back to them?

That two-day creative gathering spawned a second and a third gathering, and then more.

Now we've collected some of the songs, stories, and conversations here for you.

Join us in the circle, and in the continuing story.

We are one.

RAHAB

God's Faithfulness in Our Professions

LISTEN ALONG

"God Above, God Below (Rahab's Lullaby)"

I've always wanted to be known for something.

For the longest time, it was knowledge. I wanted to be an ivy-league-caliber professor in a small college setting, known for caring too deeply about my students and humbly publishing well-received papers at the intersection of religion and literature. I wanted to be known for my love of words and books and learning, and I wanted to inspire that love in others too.

I was one credit and a thesis shy of getting my master's degree when David and I got engaged, and I paused my MA to become a Mrs. It's true that I could have gone back to finish the work at any time, but it's hard to hop back onto a moving train once you've jumped off, especially when you're carrying a twin boy on each hip and chasing a toddler girl who's three going on thirteen.

> ## "Why couldn't I be the kind of together mom I imagined I should be?"

I never got back on the grad school train, but my dream—the one the world told me it was my right to chase—was replaced with something new before I knew it. Next, it was Pinterest-worthy parenting. The kids and I stayed home all day every day, save for the magical six hours a week they were in Mother's Day Out. We read a million books and played silly games, had dance parties in the kitchen, and made forts out of sofa cushions. We went to the park—the nearest one with a fenced-in playground because two toddlers and a five-year-old can be terribly difficult to keep safe when cars are nearby—and the library, friends' houses, and Costco (for the double-seater shopping cart, free food samples, and high, noise-absorbing ceilings). I made homemade learning toys out of paint chips and clothespins, plastic bins and buttons. It looked pretty impressive from a distance. But the reality was that each day was a struggle, and anxiety was taking root in my mind and body. Why couldn't I be the kind of together mom I imagined I should be?

I've held a variety of jobs in my life. middle school youth intern, customer care coordinator, financial aid administrator, proofreader, editor, author, executive. And I've aspired to countless other labels along the way: praiseworthy daughter, all-star employee, inspirational leader, devoted wife, and wise-beyond-her-years friend, to name a handful. As truly good as these aspirations may be, none of them alone seems to sum up a life. I'm still a wonderfully complicated mess of a human; even the labels I want the most don't always stick.

> ## *"A person's work and identity aren't the same thing, are they?"*

Perhaps this is the reason the question "So, what do you do?" lands awkwardly on my ears. A person's work and identity aren't the same thing, are they? Even so, it's become our default, trying to understand one another by first asking which worldly labels fit, which categories claim us. As followers of Jesus, we too are guilty of misplacing our identity, putting so much emphasis on the calling that we forget that the story and glory belong to the God who calls.

Do you think this has always been true? I wonder if we were to ask, "So, what do you do?" to the men and women in Scripture, would they answer with their profession? Nehemiah's role was cupbearer to the king. Some of the disciples made their living as fishermen. Paul made tents. Jesus was a carpenter, Zacchaeus was a tax collector, and David was a shepherd before he was a king. Lydia was a retailer of purple cloth. Is this who they were?

Rahab was a woman in the Old Testament whose profession seemed synonymous with her identity. "Rahab the prostitute" she is called in the text, the label indelibly linked to her name. Even in the original Hebrew language, the word here meant what you'd assume it means: harlot, prostitute, or perhaps keeper of an inn where this type of transaction took place. Commentaries have not exactly been kind to Rahab over the years, calling her names like "shady lady," "lady of the night," and the like. But is Rahab's profession the truest thing there is to know about her? More importantly, is it the way God knows her?

When we read Rahab's story, starting in *Joshua 2*, we find that the centerpiece of Rahab's story is a different kind of profession—not her line of work but her profession of faith: *"The LORD your God is God in heaven above and on the earth below,"* the harlot proclaimed, thus identifying herself with Yahweh, the God of Israel *(v. 11)*. As with the turning point of any good story, we have to widen our lens to understand its impact.

Rahab was a Canaanite woman living in Jericho. Her home was in the wall of the city, a common place for the scandalized and marginalized to dwell. Meanwhile, on the other side of the Jordan River, the Israelite leader Joshua, successor to Moses, was preparing to lead God's people across the river and into the city to lay claim to the land God promised their ancestors. The land of Canaan was enemy territory, but not for long. The Israelites believed the centuries-old promise that it would soon belong to them.

"She was acting on what she professed to believe."

As a woman living in this enemy territory, Rahab's loyalty was to Jericho's king. But when two Israelite spies came to scout the land, she hid them in her home and facilitated their daring escape, saving them from sure death at the hand of her people's king. Why would Rahab do this? Why risk her life for the sake of these two men?

Rahab had heard the stories of Israel's God—how He dried the waters of the Red Sea so that His people could walk free from hundreds of years of slavery, how His justice destroyed the wicked. She'd heard how this God had given His people the land of Canaan—Rahab's home—before they'd even lifted a finger to seize it. And she believed it. She believed it all. With conviction, Rahab professed her faith in Yahweh to the Israelite spies:

———

I know that the LORD has given you this land and that a great fear of you has fallen on us, so that all who live in this country are melting in fear because of you. We have heard how the LORD dried up the water of the Red Sea for you when you came out of Egypt, and what you did to Sihon and Og, the two kings of the Amorites east of the Jordan, whom you completely destroyed. When we heard of it, our hearts melted in fear and everyone's courage failed because of you, for the LORD your God is God in heaven above and on the earth below. (vv. 9–11)

———

Rahab's profession of faith declared her belief in who God is—God of heaven and earth. It declared her belief in what God had done—miraculously delivered His people from slavery and to the Promised Land. And it declared her belief in what He had the power to do—save her and her family. She followed her profession with a plea:

———

Now then, please swear to me by the LORD that you will show kindness to my family, because I have shown kindness to you. Give me a sure sign that you will spare the lives of my father and mother, my brothers and sisters, and all who belong to them—and that you will save us from death. (vv. 12–13)

———

By risking her life to save the spies, Rahab put her life in Yahweh's hands, thereby surrendering her life to Him, the one true God.

This is a stunning act of faith by any measure. And the Scripture writers recognize it as such. The harlot turned hero, Rahab, appears in the "hall of faith" in Hebrews 11, listed with the likes of Noah, Sarah, Jacob, and Moses as one *"approved through their faith"* (v. 39 CSB).

But here's what gets me: Rahab wasn't trying to be a hero. She was just trying to be obedient. She was living out her newly found faith.

Rahab's faith didn't end with her knowledge or stop at her words. It manifested itself in action. Faith for Rahab looked like taking in two spying strangers who came to her home at the edge of the city. It looked like moving some stalks of flax to cover them as they lay still on the rooftop, knowing that if they were discovered, they'd all three be killed by the king. We look back now and see these as big, bold acts of faith, and they were. But to Rahab, they were the next right thing. She was acting on what she professed to believe.

Could this Canaanite have dreamed she'd be in the very lineage of the Messiah? Could she have known that she would be one of two examples of living faith given by James in his now-famous treatise on faith and works? Faith in theory alone is not faith at all, James explains *(chapter 2)*. Even the demons believe in the one true God. Faith in practice is the thing. And what does real faith—dynamic faith—look like? According to James, it looks like Abraham laying his son on the altar and Rahab risking everything to hide the spies. Rahab, one of the most unexpected examples of faith in the Bible, appears alongside Abraham, an ancient father of the faith. Did Rahab know this was her calling, or was she simply following the lead of the God who calls?

To have a faith without works didn't seem to occur to Rahab. She proclaimed that Yahweh was God, and if a person proclaims something that huge, doesn't it make sense to act on it? If I profess faith in the one true God, shouldn't I shape my life around that faith? Like Abraham before her, Rahab was an ordinary person who believed in God and acted like it.

"By risking her life to save the spies, Rahab put her life in Yahweh's hands, thereby surrendering her life to Him, the one true God."

But there is something about Rahab's story that I find even more compelling than her unabashed faith in action. I love how her story points me straight to Jesus.

When Rahab asked the spies to return her kindness and *"save alive"* her family *(Joshua. 2:13 ESV)*, the men gave her some very specific instructions:

———

Behold, when we come into the land, you shall tie this scarlet cord in the window through which you let us down, and you shall gather into your house your father and mother, your brothers, and all your father's household. Then if anyone goes out of the doors of your house into the street, his blood shall be on his own head, and we shall be guiltless. But if a hand is laid on anyone who is with you in the house, his blood shall be on our head. (v. 18–19 ESV)

———

The scarlet cord was a symbol to the Israelites that Rahab and her family were inside, and their lives were spared the destruction that fell on the rest of the city. Like the blood-marked doorposts of the first Passover, the scarlet cord meant salvation, pointing forward to the blood of Jesus Christ, the ultimate and last Passover lamb. *"Our life for yours even to death!"* the spies had said to Rahab *(v. 2:14 ESV)*. In their cry we hear echoes of Jesus Himself: *"Greater love has no one than this: to lay down one's life for one's friends" (John 15:13)*. And so a short time after the Israelites celebrated Passover on the plains outside Jericho, Joshua led God's people to march around the city. On day seven, the walls fell and Israel destroyed the inhabitants of Jericho. But they passed over the home of Rahab, the scarlet cord gleaming in her window. Because of Rahab's faith and because of Yahweh's mercy, she and her family were "saved alive," a profound foreshadowing of the blood of Jesus, by which we too are saved.

∾

This is why Rahab's profession of faith inspires me so: When we know who's writing the story, we can see evidence of Him at every turn. We don't have to manufacture our own plotline or chase after our significance. When we know who's writing the story—the God of heaven above and earth below—we begin to understand that all parts of the narrative—large and small, seen and unseen—are powerful and purposeful.

Rahab's part in the grand story of redemption was not a product of her planning or striving. She did not determine to work her way into the history book of God's people. She simply made a statement of faith and then acted on it. The power of Rahab's profession of faith was not found in herself but in the God whose power she proclaimed and to whose sovereign will she surrendered her life.

I don't want a useless faith. I want a dynamic faith—the kind of living, active faith that speaks loudest without words. I want to be less concerned with being known for doing something great for God and more concerned with making God's greatness known. I want my primary profession—my life's work—to be living out the faith I profess with my lips.

I'm learning that a life of faithfulness does not look the way we dream it might. It's richer, fuller, more surprising than that. Rarely do I feel I'm given one big assignment from the Lord, one shining opportunity to show myself faithful. Instead, I find a million little moments—endless chances to proclaim with my actions what I profess with my words.

It happens in that moment when my children—who now number four instead of three—barrel into the room without warning, pushing my thought train off its track and frustrating my efforts to focus. Will I push them away with my body language, refusing to be interrupted? Or will I imitate the humility of Jesus, who refused to see children as interruptions?

It happens on days when my heart is heavy and I want to believe the worst of the world. Will I give myself over to indifference, sitting passively in despair while claiming I'm waiting for the kingdom to come? Or will I embrace the truth I say I believe, asking and expecting God to work in my community, my country, and my world, starting with my own heart? Will I model my posture after Jesus, humbling myself to listen when I would rather speak, serve when I would rather be served?

When the alarm goes off too early tomorrow and I slink to the kitchen to crush pills and draw up medicines in colorful syringes for my beloved youngest child, will I wish our life had led me somewhere other than this ordained, ordinary moment? Or will I see it for the lavish gift of grace that it is?

No one calls me Professor, and I'm still not a model parent. But I'm coming to understand that a life of great faith is not so easily labeled anyway.

Like Rahab, our title is not our identity. Our dreams do not define us. The God of heaven above and earth below is the author of our story and the giver of our worth. He has created us in His image and commissioned us to carry that image into the world, proclaiming the goodness, mercy, and power of the one true King.

I like to imagine the rest of Rahab's story, how her faith must have deepened over time and how her knowledge of and affection for Yahweh grew as she continued to live her one wild, precious life for Him. What stories did she tell her baby boy, Boaz *(Matt. 1:5)*, and how did they shape him into a man of faith? Was she still alive to see how he would welcome a foreigner named Ruth into the family of God, the same way she had been welcomed a generation before? Did she know how her faith would come to inspire the hearts of God's daughters for lifetimes to come, teaching them that their past does not define their future?

I like to imagine her as an old woman, smiling to see some of the divine ruckus she had caused: Rahab the prostitute. Smuggler of spies. Mother of the faith. Beloved child of God. If she ever wanted to be known for something, I think she got her wish.

God, our Father and King, thank You for giving us Rahab's story. Thank You for teaching us that our first calling is to profess our faith in You, not just with our words but with our lives. We praise You for the gift of faith, for opening our eyes to see You as You are—God of heaven above and earth below and everything between. We praise You for the gift of Jesus, the Lamb of God whose sacrifice brings us eternal life. We praise You for the gift of Your Word, a record of the story of redemption You are writing. May we make our lives only about this: who You are, what You have done, and what You will do. In Your holy name we pray.

Amen.

ABOUT THE AUTHOR

Amanda Bible Williams

Amanda Bible Williams is cofounder and chief content officer of She Reads Truth. A lover of words and the Word, Amanda spends her days reading and leading, writing and editing, and explaining that her maiden name really is Bible. She lives with her husband and their four children in a chaotic farmhouse just south of Nashville, Tennessee.

"WHEN WE *know who's WRITING* THE STORY, WE CAN SEE *EVIDENCE* OF HIM *at* EVERY TURN."

— *Amanda Bible Williams*

L to R: Ruth Chou Simons, Raechel Myers

RUTH

God's Faithfulness in Our Disillusion

LISTEN ALONG

"We Are One"

God's faithfulness isn't based on my current set of circumstances. At least, I know this intellectually. His inherent goodness doesn't ebb and flow along the shoreline of how well my life is going, or not. But I sure do feel better about Him when spring is in the air, my relationships are thriving, and I have reservations at Margot's (the coziest restaurant in town). When life is sure-footed and happy, I suppose it's easier to get behind the idea that God is good. But what about when life goes the other way and the disappointments keep crashing as surely as waves hurl themselves onto the shore? When you've just scraped the sand out of your bathing suit and another crest douses you from behind and down you go again? What is God like then? Is He faithful and good in all circumstances? And if so, what are we to make of that seemingly dichotomous pairing: the pain of life and the faithfulness of God? The book of Ruth may not give us a simple answer, but it offers an undeniable narrative of our Redeemer.

When I was twenty-five, I moved from my home of northern Virginia to Nashville, Tennessee. My gunmetal-gray Jeep Cherokee puffed and fumed down I-81 South, stuffed with clothes, a few small pieces from my parents' house (where I'd been living), my guitar, and dreams hanging out of every window. I'd slid my whole life's worth of chips into the middle of the table, except nothing about that move felt like gambling. Rather, I was going all-in on my one dream: becoming a singer-songwriter. I had big plans to be wildly successful, all for the glory of God, of course. A few years later, my business manager neatly described things when she leaned toward me over a restaurant table, folded her hands, and said, "I've never seen anything not work this much." And just like that, my music career and the better part of my twenties were captured in a sentence.

> ## *"Every break seemed to be a bad one instead of the big one."*

She wasn't mistaken. I felt everything go dismally wrong to the specificity of a crossed *t* and dotted *i*. It was as if God Himself was thwarting my path. From the very beginning, people who signed me to record deals lost their jobs shortly thereafter, the companies I signed with got sold or went under, merchandise was shipped to the wrong warehouse before a major tour, and nearly every sure thing turned into "Well, we've never had anything like *this* happen before." Every break seemed to be a bad one instead of a big one. Eventually I found myself years down the road with three failed record deals, living alone, squeezed financially, and not a thing to show for my efforts—except a *spectacular* plaque from a short-lived number-one hit on Christian radio. I was anxious. Purpose eluded me as much as the dreams I was seeking. All the while, I wondered why God seemingly tricked me into coming to Nashville. I thought I was following Him, albeit my priorities were a tad out of whack.

> *"The book of Ruth is one of the most compelling redemption stories in Scripture, and perhaps of all time."*

While I may not have used such piercing language, I identified with the words of Ruth's mother-in-law, Naomi:

"The LORD's hand has turned against me!" (Ruth 1:13). Without in any way setting my nontragic disappointments next to Naomi's loss of a husband and two sons or Ruth's loss of a husband, I identified with Naomi's conclusions about God's relationship to her life. I hadn't felt God's wind at my back for quite some time; rather, He felt more like a blustering gust into which my path always seemed to be headed. I suppose I didn't recognize at the time that even this was a sign of His presence. During those days (and since), the book of Ruth became a well-worn park bench where I could sit beside old friends who, despite the blowing uncertainty around them, found God to be nothing less than wholly faithful. But this took time, of course, for all of us.

The book of Ruth is one of the most compelling redemption stories in Scripture, and perhaps of all time— at least in my humble opinion. Like most good stories, it begins with complications and even tragedy in desperate need of restoration. Famine plagued Bethlehem, most likely due to the Israelites' collective waywardness toward God. So an Israelite family of four—Elimelek; his wife, Naomi; and their two sons, Mahlon and Kilion— left God's chosen town for the distant pagan land of Moab. Rather than stay and suffer for a season with the people of God, the family chose to flee the place of His presence for fuller bread baskets. The problem was that to dwell in Moab was to dwell with a people whose hearts were far from Israel's God.

Sometime after the family's relocation to Moab, Elimelek died. In an ultimate blow to Naomi's heart and future well-being, both her sons died as well, sometime after marrying Ruth and Orpah. In Israelite society, a woman's significance and sustenance were wrapped up in the life of her husband, who provided, and her sons, who carried on the family name and legacy. So here our drama begins with Naomi, a childless widow with two foreign daughters-in-law (Ruth and Orpah), who are now also widowed. Three grieving women take center stage, one with rich Israelite heritage, and two with Moabite blood running through their veins. Despite Moab being a land at odds with Israel and Naomi having fled Bethlehem, neither was beyond God's *hesed*. But we'll get to that word in a moment.

It's funny the things we can still hear from and about God when we're in far-off places. I wouldn't have expected Naomi to be able to hear anything about Israel's God since she and her husband made their beds far away in the land of false gods. I would have assumed God's grace and provision were only for the people who stayed in Bethlehem and endured the famine. In other words, the people who "earned" it. Additionally, when we stray from the sheep pen, how far can the Shepherd's voice be expected to travel? Well, apparently it can reach all the way to a place like Moab:

———

When Naomi heard in Moab that the LORD had come to the aid of his people by providing food for them, she and her daughters-in-law prepared to return home from there. (Ruth 1:6)

———

When the peals of God's grace rang out in Moab, the echoes of invitation extended all the way to Naomi and her Moabitess daughters-in-law. Naomi prayed that Yahweh, the God of Israel, would show faithful love or "kindness" to Ruth and Orpah as He had shown it to her *(see v. 8)*. The Hebrew word for this selfless and unconditional love is *hesed*, and it's based on covenant—not on one's ability to earn it. Scholar Daniel I. Block speaks of it this way: "Israel associated it with Yahweh's covenant relationship with her; that is, despite her waywardness, Yahweh always stood steadfastly by Israel in 'covenant loyalty'."[1]

We may be tempted to think that

such an Old Testament term is meant for Old Testament times. But in fact, the *hesed* of God culminates in the person of Jesus. His unconditional love rings out today—all the way to the furthest reaches of our sin and wandering. And when such an invitation reaches our hearts, we should do as Naomi and her daughters-in-law did: start the journey home.

Somewhere along that formidable trek, Orpah decided to turn back, but Ruth clung to Naomi. Right before their parting, the narrator describes the three of them weeping together loudly *(v. 14)*. While we all weep in this life, the direction in which we weep makes all the difference. Orpah wept backward to the familiar, her pagan gods, and away from the one true God of Israel. But Ruth and Naomi wept forward. This scene particularly moves me as a reminder to keep my feet pointed toward the Lord even when what He's asking of me brings immeasurable tears. My obedience to Him as a single woman, as a disciple, has often been costly. When I reflect on Jesus' commands in Scripture—the high call of loving others, forgiving, letting go of bitterness, putting on compassion, kindness, humility, and dying to my selfish desires and ambitions ... well, it's a radical way of life. At the same time, it's borne fruit I never would have tasted had I clung to what I thought I

needed for life and happiness over what He revealed I needed from His Word.

My own path has been far from linear, but I've discovered that a nonlinear path often results in linear sanctification. In other words, when I can't make sense of what God is doing and I'm zigzagging in directions I don't fully understand, my path to Christ becomes surprisingly straight. Anything I've suffered in my life has drawn me closer to Him if I've allowed it to. And I've discovered that being transformed into the image of Christ is infinitely more valuable than the personal achievements I accomplish along the way *(2 Cor. 3:18)*.

A few years after my arrival in Nashville, I remember sitting in that same Jeep, which had inadvertently become like a sanctuary to me—a lot of praying, tears, and working things out transpired while driving that vehicle around. For some reason on that particular day, I sat parked in my driveway while the sky unleashed a heavy rain. I knew I needed to make a choice: to surrender and stop fighting God. In a distinctive moment, I relinquished my music career to Him, released the unhealthy relationships that weren't pleasing to Him, loosened my grip on the allure of being well-known and liked, and began to trust Him as my Provider when income was minuscule and spotty. It killed me to place all that was precious to me in the hollow of His hands, but some parts of me needed to die so they could come back new. I wept. But I wept toward Him, and that has made all the difference.

> *"I've discovered that being transformed into the image of Christ is infinitely more valuable than the personal achievements."*

Orpah's tears fell on the road back to Moab while Naomi's and Ruth's marked their way to Bethlehem, the place of God's presence and provision. With courage and poetry, Ruth declared that wherever Naomi went, she would go; where Naomi lived, she would dwell beside her; where Naomi died, she would be buried; Naomi's people would be her people; most significant of all, Naomi's God would be Ruth's God. Despite Ruth's unspeakable heartbreaks—losing her husband, parting with Orpah, leaving a homeland, and dealing with Naomi's bitterness (she was no plate of gingersnaps)—Ruth cried her tears toward the God of Israel. And in a stunning extension of *Deuteronomy 23:3* (no Moabite could enter the assembly of the Lord), Ruth the Moabitess found shelter under the wings of the God of Israel *(Ruth 2:12)*.

When Naomi and Ruth arrived at the city gates of Bethlehem—Naomi after at least ten years away and Ruth for the first time—they did so during a specific event the author makes sure we don't miss. They *"arriv[ed] in Bethlehem as the barley harvest was beginning" (1:22)*. To our modern ears a barley harvest doesn't have quite the thrilling ring of, say, the beginning of an economic boom, a Maui vacation, or a coffee-bean bumper crop. But stalks of barley as far as the eye could see, swaying in the wind, tangibly expressed God's provision and love for the people of Israel—and for a Moabitess named Ruth. Provision they could hold, reap, and consume.

That Ruth and Naomi arrived at the beginning of the harvest meant God had been working before their arrival. He had been conducting an obscure underground operation of preparing seeds that unfolded and shot through the soil into daylight—at just the right time. He was way ahead of Naomi and Ruth, something they were just starting to realize. And in a shocking twist, it turns out the beginning of the barley harvest had a little to do with barley and a lot more to do with Boaz. The man who owned the field in which Ruth gleaned was also the family's kinsman-redeemer. One day he would become Ruth's husband, they would have a son named Obed, both Naomi's and Ruth's lives and legacy would be redeemed, and all would find their place in the genealogy of King David and Jesus Christ.

> *"You are my Redeemer, the one who restores and who works all things out for the good of those who love You."*

My story isn't nearly this epic. After several years of being in Nashville, I remember I'd occasionally run into people in places like the grocery store and they'd say, "Oh hey, I didn't know you still lived here!" I suppose the only reason I still did was because God was working out His path and purpose for me, even if it was barely visible to the naked eye. God does so much of His best work beneath the soil.

While it's easy to question God's goodness and faithfulness in the midst of loss, tragedy, or a simple string of disappointments, Ruth's story has this phenomenal way of showing us that our dead ends aren't God's. While our losses leave hollow craters in our hearts, He has the ability to bring something from nothing. When we cry out like Naomi, *"I went away full, but the LORD has brought me back empty,"* He has a way of sticking a Ruth by our side *(1:21)*. When all Naomi saw was the shameful tie of a Moabitess daughter-in-law clinging to her coattails, only God saw that Ruth would one day be worth more to her than seven sons *(4:15)*, the perfect number of completeness in Israelite culture.

Had God's hand truly gone out against Naomi, or was He drawing her into a story of redemption the likes of which found its culmination in the coming of Jesus Christ? Was Ruth a forsaken and widowed Moabitess who would always be seen as less than a foreign servant girl *(2:13)*, or would God give her a place among the matriarchal heroes of Israel *(4:11)*? We know the answers to these questions in hindsight, but in the moment, Ruth could only see barley to be gleaned for survival, and Naomi could only taste her own bitterness. God redeemed both of their stories in unfathomable fashion. And He is capable of doing the same for us.

I don't believe life is a series of misfortunes that in some strange way turn out to be enormous blessings if we only trust God. That would be entirely too simplistic, not to mention a dismissal of real loss and tragedy, evil, and plain suffering. Yet I fully believe we can cling to the truth that our God is able to take that which was meant for evil and turn it into good, as was the case with Joseph and his brothers in Genesis 50:20. I believe He gathers the difficult things in our lives and works them together for the good of those who love Him and are called according to His purpose, as Paul describes in Romans 8:28. I believe His supernatural hands are still capable of restoring the years the locusts have eaten *(Joel 2:25)*. I believe Jesus has inaugurated a new age in His kingdom that makes all things new, not the least of which is us *(2 Cor. 5:17)*.

When you arrive at the end of the book of Ruth, you don't just walk away with a sense of God's unfathomable ability to redeem and restore but also a grander idea of who He is. He is present and active in our stories, not only when we can't see or feel Him but also when what we feel doesn't appear to fit His nature at all. He is sovereign in all things, and the more we follow Him, the more precious this surety becomes. He is full of mercy for the widow, foreigner, and grieving. He is gracious to call the wayward and outcast home. Perhaps most significant, God is the good and faithful author of His grand story of redemption that cannot be thwarted by our own losses, disappointments, or sin.

Somewhat oddly, this story ends with a genealogy. Centuries later, Matthew 1 completed the genealogy of Jesus Christ, and the connection became obvious. The *hesed* God showed to Israel, and to Ruth the Moabitess, culminated in Jesus, the ultimate Kinsman-Redeemer, who laid His life down for us, took our sin and shame upon Himself on the cross, rose from the dead, and adopted us into His family.

Nearly two decades have passed since making my way to Nashville, since the rejection and disappointment of ailing ventures and lost dreams. So many tangible parts of my life have changed for the better. I still get to write songs, but mostly I write books and Bible studies, rich blessings I didn't see coming. Performing morphed into teaching and speaking, and in retrospect, I find this outlet more suited to my personality. I am still single, which has its blessings and trials. But my young nieces and nephew live just a few miles away, and their little lives have "renewed" and "sustained" me the way baby Obed is described as having done for Naomi *(4:15).*

I am exceedingly thankful for my closest friends, who are dynamic and who love and seek the heart of Christ. I have a rich church community, and I'm grateful daily for my family. Tomato seedlings are growing in my garden beds, flourishing under the sun and showers of late spring. And my neighbor's little girl frequently visits me on my front porch and asks me a million questions I can't possibly answer while we drink cherry juice concoctions out of special cups.

My life is peaceful but not perfect. It is full but not always complete. I have my heartaches and unmet longings. But I have found God to be faithful, not only because of what He's done for me, but mostly because of who He is. His character remains true in good times and challenging ones. I cannot make full sense of the suffering and tragedy that happens in life, but I know we have a Kinsman-Redeemer who shares in our suffering and will one day return to make all things new. Until then, I will take my cue from Ruth and find refuge under His wings.

L to R: Sarah Macintosh,
Kelly Minter, Lisa Harper

Dearest Jesus, my Kinsman-Redeemer, thank You that I can take refuge under Your wings. I am here not because of my heritage, status, or righteousness but because Your sacrifice and love have made a place for me. Though I am grieving loss, or disappointed that my life hasn't turned out like I thought it would, or disillusioned by Your hand seeming as though it is against me—I choose to trust You. I confess that You are good, faithful, and true in every conceivable way. I surrender all I hold dear to Your keeping. Though I may weep, I will weep forward by Your side. For You are my Redeemer, the one who restores and who works all things out for the good of those who love You. Hide me under the safety and shelter of Your wings, for in You I take refuge.

Amen.

ABOUT THE AUTHOR

Kelly Minter

Kelly Minter is passionate about teaching the Bible and believes it permeates all of life. When she's not writing, singing, or speaking, you can find her picking homegrown vegetables in her garden, cooking for her family and friends, enjoying her six nieces and nephews, or riding a boat down the Amazon River in Brazil with Justice & Mercy International (justiceandmercy.org). To read more about Kelly's adventures in the Amazon, you can pick up her book *Wherever the River Runs*, or if you love cooking, you can find her cookbook called *A Place at the Table*. For a deeper study into the book of Ruth, Kelly wrote a Bible study called *Ruth: Loss, Love & Legacy*. And her latest study—*Finding God Faithful*—is on the life of Joseph.

"GOD DOES *so much of HIS* BEST WORK BENEATH *the* SOIL."

— *Kelly Minter*

Top: Trillia Newbell
Left L to R: Kelly Minter, Sarah Macintosh, Leslie Jordan,
Amanda Bible Williams, Ellie Holcomb, Keely Scott, Susan
McPherson, Christy Nockels, Ruth Chou Simons, Raechel Myers

JEHOSHEBA

God's Faithfulness in Obscurity

LISTEN ALONG

"At This Very Time"

Where is God when I'm doing dishes?

A sink full of dinner dishes screams for my attention as I sit down to write this chapter. Not even this beloved task of writing is loud enough to drown out the constant rhythm of dirtying and cleaning my kitchen. Cook. Eat. Wash. Dry. Put away. Repeat. Cook. Eat. Wash. Dry. Put away. Repeat. Cook. Eat. Wash. This is the endless loop that punctuates my life.

I counsel others and come home to a dishwasher to unload. I write articles and return to make dinner. I speak at women's events, and those soaking pans from last night greet me, reminding me that while my hands may sometimes be used to sign books, they are more often used to scrub the corners of my nine-by-thirteen-inch pan. It matters little how grandiose my wanderings are during the day; I come home to a life of unremarkable ordinariness. A life of groceries, laundry, and dishes.

And where is God in all this?

If I'm honest, He seems far more active in my Bible teaching than my dish drying. So to escape the mediocrity of those moments, I often scroll through my social media feeds. A new book releasing. Job successes. Cute clothes. International travel. A new song. Engagement pictures. A missionary update. Creative kid crafts. New blog posts. An endless loop of meaningful activities in other people's lives. I put the phone down and pick up the towel. What's a clean kitchen compared to a podcast?

> "We long to soar above the minutiae and make an impact that lasts."

Our online interconnectedness sets the achievements of others before our eyes in unprecedented ways. It awakens our desire to do something noteworthy. And our modern technology has made such noteworthy activities available to us all. Want your own radio show? Go start a podcast. Want to make music? Just download GarageBand and get going. Want to become a writer? Start a blog.

The combination of watching others "hit it big" and having the technology to pursue it ourselves throws gasoline on the fire of our desire to be world-changers. We ache for our lives to matter. We long to soar above the minutiae and make an impact that lasts. But those pesky dishes keep us tethered to the ground. If only we could break free from the mediocrity and obscurity, then our lives would matter.

EXPECTING TOO LITTLE

These repetitive and unseen tasks in my life are in such contrast to what I see online that it's hard to suppress my insecurity.

Doubts multiply as quickly as the springtime weeds. *God, are You going to use my life? Does what I do matter at all? I know raising children is a good thing, but it feels like I'm wasting my days while my husband does the important work. When are You going to use my life? Am I just in the waiting room? When will I begin the work that really matters? Are You going to be faithful through me? Or just through others?*

I'm sure you've had these questions too. Maybe they arise from your prolonged singleness. Or they crept in when your dream job crashed to the ground. Or when your marriage collapsed. Maybe, like me, they are the result of others' successes. Maybe you watched your friends jump into ministry right after college while you had a honeymoon baby. And you wonder, What's rocking babies compared to overseas missions?

Underneath it all, we just want our lives to matter. And that's a good thing! We should hope they matter! The Bible is clear we're meant to live for something bigger than just survival. In fact, Paul encourages us to live like a runner trying to win a race *(1 Cor.9:24)*!

So why do we face so much doubt and discouragement? Are we expecting too much out of life? Should we just settle into the reality that most of us will live boring, unremarkable lives that don't matter that much?

"We've shrunk the category of what is world-changing to what is Instagrammable."

No! I don't think we're expecting too much out of life. Quite the opposite: I think we're expecting too little. We've shrunk the category of what is world-changing to what is Instagrammable. If that's true, then very little of our lives is meaningful.

But when we open the pages of our Bibles, we see something surprising. God moves His kingdom forward through amazingly ordinary activities. Amid the extraordinary and miraculous stories, we find that the normative movement of God through history happens in those little moments of faith. Amid the Esthers, Ruths, and Deborahs are many lesser-known women who advance the kingdom through small acts of faith and obedience.

"Obscure doesn't mean insignificant."

As I've studied my Bible, it's these lesser-known women whom I've clung to. It's these women who have strengthened my faith the most. One such woman is my friend Jehosheba. May I introduce her to you?

A COURAGEOUS AND SELFLESS AUNT

The only remarkable thing about Jehosheba was the monstrous family she found herself in. Not only was she related to Jezebel, the most well-known villainess of the Bible, but her own father murdered all his brothers out of his hunger for power. In fact, at first glance, Jehosheba appears to be of such small account in this dark moment of Judah's history that many people miss her altogether. I've talked to many well-read Bible students who have no idea who she is.

But obscure doesn't mean insignificant. Let's read her story:

———

When Athaliah the mother of Ahaziah saw that her son was dead, she proceeded to destroy the whole royal family. But Jehosheba, the daughter of King Jehoram and sister of Ahaziah, took Joash son of Ahaziah and stole him away from among the royal princes, who were about to be murdered. She put him and his nurse in a bedroom to hide him from Athaliah; so he was not killed. He remained hidden with his nurse at the temple of the LORD for six years while Athaliah ruled the land.
(2 Kings 11:1–3)

———

So if your head is spinning from all those strange names (Atha-who?), hang with me. We'll break it down together. The first player in this moment in history was Athaliah, Jehosheba's stepmother.

Athaliah was the daughter of a king, a wife to a king, and the mother of a king. But apparently, being in the royal family was not enough. In this moment, her son—King Ahaziah—had died. And rather than mourning, she saw the death of her own son as an opportunity to seize power for herself. To prevent any rightful heir to reign in his place, she began killing *"the whole royal family."* Now think for a moment. Who is the royal family? It's *her* family! These are her very own children and grandchildren!

It's in this family massacre that we see our heroine, Jehosheba, emerge. Consider for a moment the fear and confusion of being hunted by your own relative, watching her kill off your family in the wake of your brother's death. Whom would you trust? What would you do in the face of such evil? Very few of us have faced such a moment.

Despite the risks, Jehosheba acted to benefit someone other than herself, saving her one-year-old nephew, Joash, and his nurse from the line of fire. But she didn't just spare him from death and drop him off at the local orphanage. No, Jehosheba stepped into this battle for the long haul. She ensured his survival by hiding him in the one place she was sure evil Athaliah wouldn't go: the house of the Lord. And there in the temple, baby Joash stayed, hidden for six years while his power-hungry, murdering grandmother reigned over the land.

Though we aren't sure if Jehosheba lived in the temple with her nephew and his nurse for those six years, her daily involvement in his care was certain, as they would have had no means of survival without her constant provision and protection. Regardless of where she laid her head at night, Joash's life-preserving hiddenness was her responsibility.

> *"This is exactly why we need Jehosheba's story. Because we all face hidden battles. Hidden sacrifices. Hidden struggles."*

Consider the magnitude of her task: Six years. Hiding a little boy. In one building. A boy whose very existence threatened the current regime. Death awaited if they were discovered. Rarely, until COVID-19, have we understood the difficulty of raising children in confinement. It's hard to fathom what Jehosheba faced in those six years, afraid for her life with an energetic little boy to keep safe. A little boy who wasn't even her own son.

Here's the kicker: this woman risked her life, pouring herself out daily for the life of her nephew, and no one knew about it. The very nature of her task was hidden. It wouldn't have been on Facebook or Instagram. In fact, it would have appeared that she went dark. Fell off the grid. Her sacrifice completely removed her from the public square and propelled her into obscurity. And not just for a few months, but six years! What were you doing six years ago? Now imagine all that time secretly raising your nephew. This was anything but easy.

This is exactly why we need Jehosheba's story. Because we all face hidden battles. Hidden sacrifices. Hidden struggles. We have lives full of mundane challenges, like childcare and family drama. And we need a heroine to look up to who's been where we've been. Who's faced those years of difficult obscurity and daily obedience when no one was looking. We need a heroine who stands up to the Athaliah take-what-you-want-no-matter-the-cost attitude. The testimony of her life can help us endure our own seasons of sacrificial hiddenness when everyone else seems to be "ruling and reigning." But that's not the only reason we need heroes like Jehosheba.

MORE AT STAKE

Jehosheba succeeded in keeping little Joash hidden (a truly miraculous feat, as any boy mom can attest) and helped bring an end to Athaliah's rage. With the help of her husband, the priest, and the army, Joash was anointed the rightful king at seven years old.

———

In the seventh year Jehoiada [Jehosheba's husband] showed his strength. He made a covenant with the commanders of units of a hundred....

Jehoiada and his sons brought out the king's son and put the crown on him; they presented him with a copy of the covenant and proclaimed him king. They anointed him and shouted, "Long live the king!"

When Athaliah heard the noise of the people running and cheering the king, she went to them at the temple of the LORD. She looked, and there was the king, standing by his pillar at the entrance. The officers and the trumpeters were beside the king, and all the people of the land were rejoicing and blowing trumpets, and musicians with their instruments were leading the praises. Then Athaliah tore her robes and shouted, "Treason! Treason!"

Jehoiada the priest sent out the commanders of units of a hundred, who were in charge of the troops, and said to them: "Bring her out between the ranks and put to the sword anyone who follows her." For the priest had said, *"Do not put her to death at the temple of the LORD."* So they seized her as she reached the entrance of the Horse Gate on the palace grounds, and there they put her to death. *(2 Chron. 23:1, 11–15)*

———

Finally! This terror of a woman was gone from Judah. But the good news didn't stop there. If you keep reading, you'll see that Jehosheba's courage ushered in a sweet season for God's people. After Athaliah was put to death, a new covenant was made between the Lord, Joash, and the people, *"that they would be the LORD's people"* (2 Kings 11:17).

The idolatrous temple of Baal was destroyed. And the Bible ties a bow on this chapter with this telling phrase: *"The people of the land rejoiced, and the city was calm" (v. 20).* Because of one woman's hidden sacrifice for the life of one child, peace was restored to an entire nation.

But there's even more beauty in Jehosheba's story than the life of this one child and the well-being of the nation.

You see, God made a promise years before Jehosheba and Joash took up hiding. A very important promise that Jehosheba may not even have been aware of. A promise made to one of Israel's first kings, King David:

———

When your days are over and you rest with your ancestors, I will raise up your offspring to succeed you, your own flesh and blood, and I will establish his kingdom. He is the one who will build a house for my Name, and I will establish the throne of his kingdom forever. (2 Sam. 7:12–13)

———

The promise is echoed by the prophet Jeremiah this way: *"For this is what the LORD says: 'David will never fail to have a man to sit on the throne of Israel'"* (Jer. 33:17).

God promised to make King David's throne an eternal one. God promised that eventually, one of his physical descendants would rise up as King of Kings and rule forever. Is this story sounding familiar yet?

Then we turn to page 1 of the New Testament, and these are the first words we see: *"This is the genealogy of Jesus the Messiah the son of David, the son of Abraham"* (Matt. 1:1).

Who is the very *first* person Matthew wants us to know Jesus is related to? David. Introducing Jesus as a "son of David" was not a one-time occurrence. Here's how the angel Gabriel described Jesus to His mother, Mary:

The angel said to her, "Do not be afraid, Mary; you have found favor with God. You will conceive and give birth to a son, and you are to call him Jesus.... The Lord God will give him the throne of his father David, and he will reign over Jacob's descendants forever; his kingdom will never end." (Luke 1:30–33)

———

Jesus is the answer to God's promise back in 2 Samuel! This promise forged a precious genealogical thread between King David and Jesus Christ. And as we read the Old Testament, we see this royal line preserved, from one son to the next, to the next, as the world awaited the Messiah. Through all the ups and downs, despite all the power-hungry players and usurping of thrones, God's people held on to the hope that a final Son of David would arise to lead them. But at one very crucial moment in the story, that thread was nearly cut.

When Athaliah began killing off the royal family, she was likely not thinking of this promise. I'm sure she was driven by her own desire to reign. But with each son of David murdered, she was sawing away at the family tree of the coming Christ.

So as Jehosheba stood up to this power-hungry murderess, she did more than save Joash. She preserved the very lineage of Jesus!

Did she know that's what she was doing? Did she know that with each meal she prepared and with every diaper changed, with every exercise of patience to keep Joash quiet, she was preserving the life of the boy who carried the seed that would one day crush the head of the serpent? Likely not.

And so it is with us. What might God be up to in our ordinary, mundane existence? What plans and purposes might He be accomplishing? What things might He be preserving? We will probably never know. But Aunt Jehosheba reminds us there's more at stake in our stories than we think.

WE NEED FRIENDS LIKE THESE

There are other women hiding in the pages of our Bibles whose ordinary actions changed the world. Women like Abigail, who, although she was married to a foolish drunkard, didn't become unwise and bitter in response but sacrificially intervened with wisdom to solve a conflict created by her husband. Her problem-solving and peace-making skills saved her family and preserved the reputation of King David.

Or what about Puah and Shiphrah, the two single women in Exodus who were the Jewish midwives? Though the most powerful man in the world commanded them to kill the babies they delivered, they simply continued to do their job. Risking their own deaths, they defended the lives of babies not born to them. And because of their obedience, the future deliverer of the enslaved people survived: Moses.

Or there's Elizabeth, the less-famous pregnant woman of Christmas. Both a pastor's daughter and pastor's wife, she lived through decades of infertility. But through those years of unfulfilled longings, miraculously she didn't grow bitter. Even in her old age, God said of her that she was blameless. And her commitment to personal holiness in the secrecy of her own heart prepared her to carry in her body the very forerunner of Jesus, a baby filled with the Holy Spirit from the womb.

Each of these women faced the temptations we face, temptations to let our difficulties and our obscurity define and discourage us. Jehosheba had a murdering stepmother, Abigail had a drunken fool for a husband, Puah and Shiphrah had the worst timing to be midwives, and Elizabeth had the challenge of infertility. They could have embraced anger, wondering why God would put them in such unfair circumstances. They could have become self-centered and entitled. But miraculously they did not!

These women believed God to be good and worthy of their obedience. So they did the hard, daily work of ordinary obedience; they cared for nephews, resolved conflicts, went to work, and endured suffering with grace. Simple, unimpressive things that were not posted or retweeted and didn't win awards. But through these small acts of faithfulness— quietly done behind the scenes—God advanced His kingdom.

We need these women as our friends and role models. The legacy of their lives reminds us that when God decides to use someone for His kingdom, He often doesn't put that person in the limelight. For these women, He sovereignly put them in positions of hiddenness and difficulty so that, at just the right time, their faith would change the world.

What might He be doing in my life as I dry the dishes? What might He be doing in yours? Through the Word we are privileged to see what God was up to in their lives, even if we cannot yet see our own lives through this lens. We're still in the middle of our own stories. Now is not the time to figure out all the ways in which God will use us. We will only know that in eternity.

What we *can* do now is reject the world's ethos that the only meaningful work is visible, measurable, and Instagrammable. We *can* offer each moment of our lives, whether dishes or diapers or discipleship, in faithful obedience to God, because each offering of hidden obedience makes us a conduit of God's kingdom-advancing work. And we *can* trust that our God will be just as faithful to us as He was to Jehosheba.

At the end of the day, I want to be a willing-to-hide Jehosheba, not an eager-to-reign Athaliah. Don't you?

Father God, we long to live with purpose and meaning, to make our lives count. And this longing is one You instilled in us when You made us for Your glory! But, Father, we are daily sold the lie that the only meaningful life is a visible one and the only measure of success is numbers. Help us resist the urge to believe this! Protect us from being conformed to the pattern of this world, and instead, transform us by renewing our minds as we study Your Word. Thank You for how You used Jehosheba and for recording her faithfulness forever in Your Word. We want to live like her. Please use our lives to move forward Your kingdom. Remind us of how eternally valuable these small acts of faithfulness are. Give us the courage to embrace the hidden seasons of our lives, the strength to be obedient when no one is watching, and the faith to believe that You are at work in the ordinary moments in ways we cannot begin to fathom. In Jesus' name and for His glory.

Amen.

ABOUT THE AUTHOR

Kelly Needham

Photo by Charity Clayton

Kelly Needham is a servant of Jesus Christ, a student of the Bible, and chief dishwasher in her home, where she lives with her husband and three children. She is the author of *Friendish* and hopes to convince as many people as possible that nothing compares to knowing Jesus.

"THROUGH *these small acts* OF FAITHFULNESS— *QUIETLY* DONE BEHIND *the scenes* —*GOD* ADVANCED *His* KINGDOM."

— *Kelly Needham*

L to R: Leslie Jordan, Sally Lloyd-Jones

THE BENT WOMAN

God's Faithfulness in Our Pain and Disappointment

LISTEN ALONG

"You Came for Me"

You know all those faithful women in the Bible we aspire to be like? The first few who come to mind are Ruth, who was so devoted, and Esther, who was so brave, or Deborah, who was such a phenomenal leader. Although I must confess that during my early years Sarah was not one of those ancient biblical heroines who came to my mind, because the idea of buying Pampers and Depends at the same time wasn't appealing to me. Little did I know then that at the age of fifty—in the very same season that AARP started mailing me membership cards and my lady-parts doctor informed me that I was running slap out of estrogen—I would become a mom through the miracle of adoption!

During our roller coaster of an adoption story, God made His redemptive presence unmistakable in so many chapters. But none were more colorful than the first bathroom bonding moment I had with my little girl, Melissa "Missy" Price Harper. The village Missy is from in Haiti is pretty primitive. At that time, only a few toilets supported fifteen hundred people, so most of the villagers used latrines. This probably sounds a bit unpleasant if you're a first-world reader, but I soon learned that indoor-plumbing avoidance is a wise, learned strategy for rural Haitians. Their commodes are often connected directly to sinks, tubs, and showers in a rudimentary fashion without the necessary valves or P traps

that keep bathing water separate from other unsavory types of fluid. Plus, their septic lines are notorious for clogging, which results in a sort of Russian roulette potty scenario because you never know when the throne your rear end is resting on will erupt like a mini volcano!

> *"During our roller coaster of an adoption story, God made His redemptive presence unmistakable in so many chapters."*

Nonetheless, around lunchtime on the second day of my very first in-country visit with Missy, I decided she must surely need to "go potty," since it was 112 degrees Fahrenheit outside and I'd cajoled her into drinking at least a gallon of filtered water while we were playing in the mission courtyard. I suggested, "Come on, sweet pea, let's go inside to the bathroom." I was delighted—if not a tad proud—when Missy willingly took my offered hand and trotted along happily beside me toward the mission's only working restroom, seeming to comprehend the task ahead of her. But her merry compliance ended as soon as we got to the end of the hallway and she saw the toilet. At this point, she knit her brows together defiantly and began trying to pull her hand out of mine.

At first her toilet antipathy didn't concern me much because many of my friends' children at Missy's age in America weren't fond of toilets either. I assumed her reticence was normal. In a continued effort to calm her fear, I knelt down in front of the toilet, held Missy firmly around her tiny waist, looked directly into her beautiful brown eyes, and said soothingly, "I've got you, honey ... You're not going to fall in ... It's okay ... Mama's got you ... Please go pee-pee, baby." I wasn't sure how many of my words she understood except for the term *pee-pee*, which is the same in Creole as it is in English.

What I didn't know then is that while Missy was technically potty-trained, she wasn't accustomed to indoor facilities. Which made it all the more tragic when—just as she'd finally gotten settled, squeezed her eyes almost shut, and wrinkled her darling nose in a concentrated effort to "go"— that cantankerous toilet erupted with a

gurgling roar and shot a geyser of filthy water all over both of us! Of course, my petite daughter-to-be shrieked in terror. I snatched her up as fast as I could while slipping and sliding in my flip-flops on the wet tile floor. Missy frantically grabbed two big fistfuls of my hair as if her very life depended on it, buried her face in my neck, and began wailing pitifully. As soon as I was able to regain my balance, I began rubbing her back in slow circles while whispering slowly, "Shush, baby, I've got you. Mama's got you. It's okay. You're okay."

> *"The deepest wounds can be the very catalysts that cause us to reach toward Him."*

She stopped crying soon enough but kept her little arms and legs wrapped tightly around me. My first thought was *Oh my goodness, my baby girl's going to still be wearing Pull-Ups in college because she's bound to suffer from Posttraumatic Pee-Pee Disorder!* This was followed closely by another thought that caused the edges of my heart to curl into a smile and my eyes to well with grateful tears: *Oh my goodness, this is the first time Missy's turned to me for comfort. My soon-to-be daughter is beginning to trust me.* I will *always* remember that broken third-world toilet with fondness because it compelled Missy to lean into my embrace for the first time.

I think that tends to be the case with us and Jesus too. The broken things—difficult relationships, past trauma, and dashed dreams—that have left the deepest wounds can be the very catalysts that cause us to reach toward Him for hope and healing. There's a true story about an unnamed but oh-so-faithful woman who encounters Jesus in Luke's gospel account that poignantly illustrates this spiritual truism.

But before we dive into the text, let's consider a few details about Luke in general that add to the sociohistorical significance of this particular encounter. The first is that Luke is the only known Gentile author of Holy Writ, which highlights the fact that God's grace is accessible to every tribe, tongue, and nation.

Dr. Luke (a physician by trade) also includes more stories about women than the other three gospel accounts. His proclivity to include women, as well as to paint them in a flattering light, was highly unusual because during the first century, women were typically regarded as chattel—as something a man could *own*.

It behooves us to keep that ancient misogynistic context in mind when perusing the following passage because it serves to magnify the miracle:

———

> *On a Sabbath Jesus was teaching in one of the synagogues, and a woman was there who had been crippled by a spirit for eighteen years. She was bent over and could not straighten up at all. When Jesus saw her, he called her forward and said to her, "Woman, you are set free from your infirmity." Then he put his hands on her, and immediately she straightened up and praised God.*
>
> *Indignant because Jesus had healed on the Sabbath, the synagogue leader said to the people, "There are six days for work. So come and be healed on those days, not on the Sabbath."*
>
> *The Lord answered him, "You hypocrites! Doesn't each of you on the Sabbath untie your ox or donkey from the stall and lead it out to give it water? Then should not this woman, a daughter of Abraham, whom Satan has kept bound for eighteen long years, be set free on the Sabbath day from what bound her?"*

When he said this, all his opponents were humiliated, but the people were delighted with all the wonderful things he was doing. (Luke 13:10–17)

Several interesting details in this story aren't immediately apparent from the text. For instance, this is the last recorded time that Jesus taught in a synagogue before the crucifixion and resurrection. Which means that, for all intents and purposes, this is our Savior's incarnate swan song. Additionally, the original Greek text from which we get the English translation *"When Jesus saw her" (v. 12)* indicates that this severely stooped woman's appearance surprised Jesus. She wasn't sitting on some back pew at the beginning of His sermon but instead entered the synagogue at some point during His message. Basically, she crashed His good-bye party.

Recently I was in the Orlando airport, striding toward the bathroom while preoccupied reading a text on my phone about a sale at Pottery Barn. When I finally looked up, I was standing in front of a wall of urinals, adjacent to several startled gentlemen—in the midst of exercising their (*ahem*) spiritual gift no less—because I had accidentally barged into the men's

bathroom instead of the women's! This is essentially what happened in Luke 13, except the bent woman barged into the boy's room *on purpose!*

What do you think would compel a woman—who wasn't supposed to be in the testosterone-only synagogue section where Jesus was preaching with the double whammy of being considered ceremonially unclean because of her physical ailment—to bravely insert herself where she wasn't remotely welcome? My guess is she was so sick and tired of being sick and tired that she decided begging Jesus for help was more important than behaving in a culturally acceptable way. When it came to pursuing Jesus versus upholding protocol, she made a beeline for the Christ, well aware that her presence would surely cause the crowd to frown in disapproval, if not work their curly sideburns into a furious lather while kicking her to the curb.

Isn't it interesting how pain can prompt us to take risks we wouldn't have otherwise considered? How the desperate need to have our wounds tended to can stretch us far beyond behavioral norms?

The consensus of biblical scholarship is that the woman in Luke 13 was likely suffering from a serious case of spinal stenosis or kyphosis, and since the New Living Translation describes her as "bent double" and the Passion

Translation describes her as being "doubled over," she was surely in a lot of pain.

> *"Insecurity is not the same thing as humility. Insecurity is just narcissism wearing a more socially appropriate outfit."*

I can identify with her misery on some level because I too suffer from back pain. When I was eleven years old, one of my uncles accidentally backed over me with his car, causing five fractured vertebrae. That injury, which has been exacerbated by decades of wear and tear, led to my first major back surgery in 1997, followed by a cervical fusion a few years ago. Adding insult to injury, my doc cheerfully assured me that the resulting scar would be barely noticeable because he was going to make his incision in one of my preexisting neck *folds*! Anyway, the bottom line is that I can empathize with this chick's physical pain—as I'm sure can many of you—but I think the more important question we should ask ourselves is, Do we move toward Jesus for living hope and supernatural help when we're in pain like her? Or do we mask our pain and choose to behave in less desperate, more culturally acceptable ways?

Maybe your spine is in decent shape, but I'd be willing to bet good money that you've dealt with serious emotional pain from the disappointment, depression, grief, and anxiety that are part and parcel of living in a broken world littered with abuse and abandonment, divorce and bad diagnoses, unmet longings and deep loneliness, global pandemics and governments polarized by partisan politics, and much more. In my thirty-plus years of vocational ministry, I've met more women *inside* the church who seem to be bent over double by shame, fear, heartbreak, and depression than *outside* it. Vera Bradley Bible covers and religious platitudes may camouflage our wounds, but they don't ease the ache, do they?

Frankly, I've come to believe that religiosity (focusing on external conformity to the dos and don'ts of the Judeo-Christian belief system instead of pursuing a real relationship with Jesus Christ) compounds our pain and leaves us even more crooked than we were before we tried to cover it up. I spent way too many years believing low self-esteem and humility were the same thing. But insecurity is *not* the same thing as humility. Insecurity is just narcissism wearing a more socially appropriate outfit.

Faking it is the antithesis of faithfulness; we don't have to put ourselves down in order to praise God.

And, Lord have mercy, false humility is a whole other class of crooked! Contrary to popular belief, "I'm not worthy" isn't usually the honorable worship lyric it pretends to be. Although it's a given—an incredibly obvious and true statement—the gratuitous and all-too-often insincere chorus of "I'm not worthy" takes the focus off the One who actually is! Despite what Christian culture parades as imitable behavior, a believer with low self-esteem is not a good example of faithfulness. When we choose to stay preoccupied with our own badness, we're also choosing to forgo the redemptive joy, hope, and peace available to us in God's goodness.

Bent is not a faithful posture of humility; bent is a consequence of spiritual immaturity.

Bent may be knowing Jesus as Savior while not recognizing Him as Liberator. Bent may be dutifully singing, "He's the Lord of all," while not trusting enough to bring our unflattering *all* to Him. Bent may be trying to lug around the weight of our own sin—or someone else's, like an abusive husband or a prodigal child—instead of actually believing that Jesus took care of humanity's sin conclusively on the

> *"What a huge, revitalizing relief it is to find out that hiding our frailty from the Creator of the universe is not part of our job description!"*

cross. It doesn't matter if we've cross-stitched GRACE and hung it on our wall: when we don't choose to live faithfully and love others well in response to the unmerited favor Jesus bought us through His death and resurrection, we end up living contorted by bad theology. Conversely, if we simply let go of the pretense that we're fine or can fix ourselves and honestly run/limp/crawl toward Jesus for help, we can bellow "Adios" to a hunchbacked life forever!

Case in point:

———

When Jesus saw her, he called her forward and said to her, "Woman, you are set free from your infirmity." Then he put his hands on her, and immediately she straightened up and praised God. (Luke 13:12–13)

———

Now remember the context here: Jesus was busy preaching His farewell message. Yet He didn't scold her for interrupting; instead, He summoned her to scooch closer! Which is extraordinarily good news because I think many of us remain bent because we don't want to bother God. We swallow our pain and paste on plastic smiles in misguided attempts not to inconvenience Him. What a huge, revitalizing relief it is to find out that hiding our frailty from the Creator of the universe is *not* part of our job description!

I spent way too many years bent. Even though I trusted Jesus as my Savior when I was a little girl, I was sexually abused during that same season, which left me twisted with shame. Although I believed God had saved me from my sin, I didn't think He liked me very much. It took me a really, really long time to stand up straight. To focus more on His goodness than my badness. But when I did, *everything* changed. Of course, I'm not perfectly "fixed." I still have enough rough spots that need to be divinely smoothed to last a lifetime, but I'm freer than I ever dreamed possible. This is why I'm so passionate about helping other women encounter the unconditional love of Jesus Christ in such a transformative way that their posture shifts to emotionally healed erectness: straight shoulders, heads held high, and hearts filled with genuine joy!

One of the sweetest unfoldings I've had the delight of witnessing occurred at a retreat in the Rockies a few years ago. I got to spend a three-day weekend with a small group of women, and we grew especially close after spending lots of time together praying, giggling, and groaning en masse while hiking up trails that would have made a mountain goat grouchy. In light of the bond we forged, I felt free to do something during our last session that I don't do very often. I described some of the most painful chapters in my story, as well as how I'd finally learned to lean into God's gracious promise of healing from the shame that had plagued my heart and mind for most of my life. I talked about how important it is for us to have figurative *Ebenezers* (literally translated *"stone of help"* in *1 Samuel 7:12*, a rock symbolizing the divine assistance Jehovah gave the Israelites during battles with their enemies) to help us remember the worth we have in Christ and break the bondage of degrading lies we've believed about ourselves. Then I asked anyone who had experienced physical, emotional, or sexual abuse to stand up.

I wish I could tell you I was surprised when about half of the room stood, but sadly I wasn't. Because, again, in my experience far too many of God's image bearers don't recognize His likeness when they look in the mirror or notice His presence when they peer into the emotional debris of their past. I can tell you that for a split second I felt a smidgen of panic and thought, *Oh good night, what should I do next?* I was going from my gut and not following some disingenuous script that clearly spelled out the next step! Thankfully, in the very next instant, I calmly sensed Holy Spirit prompting me to directly speak biblical promises to every single woman standing.

So I turned to the first woman on my left—a well-spoken, successful businesswoman who'd confided to me that when she was growing up, her father consistently belittled her for not performing as well in school as her siblings—and said, "You are *not* stupid." Then I quoted *2 Timothy 1:7:*

———

For the Spirit God gave us does not make us timid, but gives us power, love and self-discipline.

———

I turned to the next woman standing—a strikingly beautiful blonde woman who'd confided to me that her ex-husband emotionally abused her for years with cruel and manipulative taunts about how unattractive she was and how without him she'd be completely alone and unloved because no other man in the world would condescend to marry her—and I said, "You are *not* ugly." Then I quoted *Psalm 139:13–14:*

———

For you created my inmost being;
*   you knit me together in my*
*   [mama's] womb.*
I praise you because I am fearfully and
wonderfully made;
*   your works are wonderful,*
*   I know that full well.*

———

And so it went, with God's Spirit using the redemptive truths of His Word to heal the freshly exposed wounds of others, until I turned my attention to a woman who was standing in the first row, just a few feet in front of me. I paused, a little taken aback because I'd come to know this woman relatively well; she was a pastor's wife as well as a respected Bible teacher and spiritual leader in their community. Our eyes held for a few seconds before I declared slowly and decisively, "Laura, You. Are. *Not*. Dirty." At which point, she gasped and covered her mouth with her hand. After I quoted *Romans 8:1, "Therefore, there is now no condemnation for those who are in Christ Jesus,"* Laura collapsed into her chair and began to weep. I thought, *Aww crud. I must've said something that intensified her wound*, and made a mental note to find her when the session was over so I could apologize.

Over the next twenty or thirty minutes, I kept speaking words of affirmation and promises from Scripture over those brave, internally bruised warriors. After I'd spoken directly to every woman who was standing, we shared a special time of worship and Communion and closed in prayer. Everyone began departing the chapel in small chattering clumps.

Except for Laura (not her real name), who edged her way over to me through the dispersing crowd. After the room quieted, she confided how she'd been sexually molested by her uncle from the age of eight until the age of sixteen. She'd taken as many

AP classes as she could in order to graduate early from high school to attend a college out of state and escape his abuse. The sorrow on her countenance lifted a little when she talked about meeting her husband, Paul, in college. About how he'd invited her to a Bible study where she met Jesus. She explained how God had used both Paul's patience and Christian counseling to help her work through those painful memories of sexual abuse. She went on to describe how grateful she was to have a solid marriage and three healthy little boys.

Then she added softly, "You know, I almost didn't stand up tonight, Lisa, because I was afraid someone might wonder if Paul had been abusive to me. Plus, I thought I was over all that. But I couldn't stop thinking about that place deep inside my soul that still feels dirty every time Paul and I are physically intimate. I realized there's a corner of my heart that's still really bent. I stood up because I want to be completely healed."

She said she was surprised when I began speaking biblical promises directly to each woman standing. I replied that I was a little surprised myself, because I hadn't planned to! We both smiled, and then Laura continued, "After you told Becky she wasn't ugly, I started praying, 'Oh God, please, *please* have Lisa tell me

I'm not dirty, because if she uses that particular word, then I'll know this isn't some emotive programming element she's conjured up but is truly coming from You.' At that very moment you turned to me and said my name—you know, I'm the only one you called by name—and said the *exact* word I asked God for you to use with me. I knew beyond a shadow of a doubt it was Him speaking directly to me. And now, for the first time I can remember in my entire life, I feel *completely* clean ... like I can finally stand up straight without any shame weighing me down."

Whether we consider the ancient woman's standing-up story in Luke or Laura's recent unfolding experience, it's obvious that God doesn't want any of His daughters to live bent lives, hobbled by shame or guilt or fear or anxiety. Instead, Jesus came to give us emotionally healed, shoulders-no-longer-stooped, heads-held-high, hearts-filled-with-genuine-joy, *abundant* lives!

Dear Jesus, we're beyond grateful that Your grace is sufficient, but we also confess that we need more faith to trust You with our hidden pain. Thank You for reminding us through our spiritual sisters' stories that Your faithfulness extends to our deepest wounds and disappointments—within the circle of Your arms is the safest place for us to heal. Please teach us how to truly linger in Your embrace, Lord.

Amen.

ABOUT THE AUTHOR

Lisa Harper

Rarely are the terms *hilarious storyteller* and *theological scholar* used in the same sentence, much less to describe the same person, but Lisa Harper is anything but stereotypical! She's been lauded as a gifted communicator, whose writing and speaking overflow with colorful pop-culture references that connect the dots between the Bible era and modern life.

Her résumé includes thirty-plus years in vocational ministry and a master's of theological studies, and she's currently working on her doctorate at Denver Seminary.

"BENT IS *not a faithful* POSTURE OF *HUMILITY*; BENT IS *a consequence* OF SPIRITUAL *immaturity.*"

— *Lisa Harper*

Top L to R: Ann Voskamp, Ellie Holcomb, Amy Grant
Right: Raechel Myers, Amanda Bible Williams

LEAH

God's Faithfulness in Rejection

LISTEN ALONG

"This Time I Will Bring Praise"

You learn a lot about someone by the way they respond to rejection.

A few years ago, I watched my husband, Troy, walk through a painful season of disappointment that affected our entire family. Both professionally and personally, he was distancing from some of the most significant relationships he had formed in his adult life. The details aren't important here, but in the course of a few short months, his whole ministry, professional, and relational world was flipped upside down as he navigated the letdown of feeling measured and found "not enough" in the eyes of a particular group of people he worked to please. He found himself alone—feeling misjudged and misunderstood—and passed over in a way that seemed unfair and unjust in relation to what he felt he contributed. He felt rejected at the deepest level, and as his wife and colaborer in these efforts, I ached with him. His rejection derailed me too and resulted in an unexpected shake-up—a change of course for our family.

In that season, he hardly slept, struggled to eat, and felt deeply wounded. And yet, I watched him take his pain to the Lord rather than accuse, disparage, or return evil for evil. Everything in me wanted to cry aloud, *"This isn't fair! We deserve better!"* But Troy insisted again and again, "The Lord wants me to learn something in this setback ... even if this is not how we expected our story to be written."

> *"The Lord wants me to learn something in this setback ... even if this is not how we expected our story to be written."*

I am no stranger to rejection, myself—of a different kind. As an immigrant, learning English and assimilating to a new way of life in America, my childhood was riddled with rejection of my almond-shaped eyes, sneers over the foreign words I spoke with my parents at the car line, and the foods we ate (fried rice instead of bologna sandwiches). I have a lingering memory of standing alone as the only Asian American girl in the room, after blonde and brunette girls were picked as dance partners at parties. You don't have to look different or be from a different country of origin to have these memories. We all have stories.

What do we do when our circumstances seem unfair? How do we respond when we're not loved in return? Misunderstood? Dismissed, rejected, or unwanted?

> ## "Sometimes I want to rewrite the stories I read in the Bible. (I can tend to think I know better than God.) The account of Leah is one."

We fight the fear of rejection by trying to prove ourselves worthy. We pretty ourselves with cosmetics, adorn ourselves with trendsetting garments, and strive to earn brownie points for doing the very best work. We were made to be seen and known for whom we were created to be. Adam and Eve knew unencumbered fellowship with their Creator, God. They felt no need to hide and didn't fear rejection until sin destroyed that fellowship and introduced shame into the world. Every form of rejection, betrayal, disappointment, or pain since has been a result of fallenness, but God has also been pursuing us and winning us back.

Sometimes I want to rewrite the stories I read in the Bible. (I can tend to think I know better than God.) The account of Leah is one.

———

Leah's eyes were weak, but Rachel was beautiful in form and appearance. Jacob loved Rachel. (Gen. 29:17–18 ESV)

———

It's a story of rejection, comparison, desire, and a search for approval. A future father-in-law who tricked and cheated a lovestruck Jacob into working seven years for a woman he didn't love and then another seven years for her sister, whom he *did*. Two sisters competed for a place of favor and fulfillment. It's a story of unmet expectations, unfulfilled longing, and seemingly unfair circumstances. Leah lacked beauty and felt unloved—this is not a description any woman wants written into her story, certainly feeling forgotten by God.

Jacob loved Leah's sister, Rachel, but Laban, his father-in-law, tricked him into marriage with both women—one marriage he wanted and one he didn't. Imagine the heartache of knowing every day that you didn't measure up, weren't favored, didn't have the heart of the man you loved. This was not a culture where women had many rights or privileges. Leah couldn't just change her circumstances. She couldn't demand her feelings be heard. She couldn't run away from her plight. The situation seemed impossible for good.

But God writes stories that demonstrate His faithfulness amid unlikeliness.

———

When the Lord saw that Leah was not loved, he enabled her to conceive, but Rachel remained childless. (v. 31)

———

The Lord saw Leah in her pain. He had compassion toward her. He showed her favor when earthly favor was missing. But as the Lord met her in her need—allowing her to bear children—she fixated on achieving her goal: to win the heart of Jacob. *"Surely my husband will love me now,"* she said *(v. 32)*. Oh, how we love to win love and favor through our good works, our good looks, and our good contributions.

I'm so prone to thinking this way—twisting my blessings into the means by which I'll get what I want:

The blessing of a job promotion.

The blessing of health.

The blessing of a misunderstanding resolved.

The blessing of an extended holiday.

The blessing of a spouse, a child, a home, a fulfilled dream.

What is it you want the most? Attention? Friends? Approval? Acceptance? Applause? Comfort? Security? You know your deepest longings.

We cry, plead, and pray for the Lord to cause change in our lives. Like Leah, we long for the answers that right the wrongs, change our circumstances, give us the outcomes we believe we deserve—the answers that fix our disappointments. It's tempting to combat our feelings of disqualification or unworthiness with more impressive deeds or better behavior. If not for Jesus, we'd still be left to our own devices—seeking to maneuver our way to the good we think we want in life.

I'm reminded of Paul's letter to the Romans. Paul wanted the believers in Rome to remember the power of how they were saved through Jesus and why they had hope through the gospel. After writing pages on God's pursuit of His people, His amazing provision of grace through the cross of Christ, and the eternal hope that is ours because of Jesus, Paul penned these words that we love to read:

————

We know that in all things God works for the good of those who love him, who have been called according to his purpose. (Rom. 8:28).

————

I'm convinced that Paul chose to spell out the details of our hope in Christ with such care so his readers wouldn't miss it: our hope in the midst of hardship is that, in Christ, Jesus doesn't just work things out for our good—He *is* our good.

God was after Leah's heart more than orchestrating her life events. And for you and me, sister: God is more interested in having our hearts than having our dreams come true.

Can you think of a time when you wanted the good that God provides more than the good in knowing God Himself?

You see, God's greater purpose in Leah's life wasn't simply to temporarily make things feel right, seem fair, or work in her favor. God had His bigger purposes in mind: to include her in His greater story of love and provision, through Jesus—the promised Savior who would come through the tribe of Judah, Leah's fourth son. God's faithfulness through Leah's submission to be used of the Lord in her unchanging circumstance brought forth the Savior, Jesus. God chose to write His redemption story through the most unlikely women—women who didn't always measure up by earthly merit or qualifications. God chose to unfold His plan through circumstances that don't always make sense to us. Sometimes it takes disappointment and surrender to discover God's favor and faithfulness.

While Leah initially sought Jacob's acceptance through child-bearing, again and again, hoping to finally secure his love, his affection, his favor—she finally fixed her eyes in a new direction after the birth of Judah:

———

This time I will praise the LORD. (Gen. 29:35)

———

The text doesn't say so, but I hear it in her response—she gave up her notions of attaining favor through what she could do or not do, who she could be or not be, or how she could measure up, and chose to turn her longings to God Himself. This time—*this time*—signifies a change, a redirection, a line in the sand. Her declaration to choose praise was a belief that the posture of her heart was more important than her position in life. Despite disappointment, despite any change in her circumstances, despite her feelings, Leah chose to praise the Lord; He is worthy and better than her desires for change.

Leah recognized in that moment what believers like you and me would only come to know centuries later:

God Himself, through Jesus, His Son, is the Good we're really after.

When God works all things together for good in the life of a believer, He is pursuing us with His good, and He alone is for a desperate and dying world. When we can't change ourselves, when we can't fix our circumstances, when we can't right the wrongs, when we can't measure up to God's standards—God faithfully rescues.

What feels like disappointment to us is often God's deliberate design for our good.

Whether that disappointment looks like rejection or feeling forgotten, I know this to be true: *the Lord wants me to learn something in this*

disappointment ... even if this is not how I expected my story to be written.

The story of Leah may not feel fair, intuitive, or purposeful to us when we encounter it in the Word, but God chooses to use her—and her story— to write His great story of redemption through our Savior, Jesus Christ. That serves to encourage us today, sisters. What seemed disappointing in that season—being Jacob's first wife but only second place in his heart— led to the lineage from which Christ was born. But our God, who wastes nothing and draws near in every season or circumstance we're in, turns our hearts from crying *This time I'll get the results I want* to *This time I will praise the Lord*.

> *"God chose to write His redemption story through the most unlikely women."*

In Christ, God changes our hearts—even when the outcome is not what we expect—so we're able to turn from loving our desires most to wanting Him above all else.

Father, we praise You. Like Leah, we choose to bring You praise, even in the midst of all that we do or don't understand about our present circumstances. You tell us in Your Word, "I will never leave you nor forsake you." Because of Christ, we have the assurance of Your presence. You comfort, sustain, and restore. You are the God who redeems the most unlikely and seemingly hopeless situations. So we thank You, God—that, in You, we need not fear loneliness or rejection. In You, we are seen, loved, held, and remembered as You write Your story for good in our lives.

Amen.

ABOUT THE AUTHOR
Ruth Chou Simons

Ruth Chou Simons is a bestselling and award-winning author, artist, entrepreneur, and speaker, using each of these platforms to spiritually sow the Word of God in people's hearts. Through her online shop at GraceLaced.com and her social media community, Simons shares her journey of God's grace intersecting daily life with word and art. Ruth and her husband, Troy, are grateful parents to six boys—their greatest adventure.

Ruth's books include *GraceLaced, Beholding and Becoming, Foundations*, and *TruthFilled*, a Bible study on the practice of preaching truth to yourself.

"WHAT *feels like* DISAPPOINTMENT *to us* IS *OFTEN God's* DELIBERATE *design* FOR *OUR GOOD.*"

— *Ruth Chou Simons*

L to R: Ginny Owens, Christy Nockels, Ellie Holcomb, Leslie Jordan, Trillia Newbell, Ruth Chou Simons, Kelly Minter, Amanda Bible Williams, Lisa Harper

EVE

There is more mercy in Christ than sin in us.

— *Richard Sibbes,* The Bruised Reed

LISTEN ALONG

"We Do Not Labor in Vain"

GENESIS 3

Now the serpent was more crafty than any of the wild animals the Lord God had made. He said to the woman, "Did God really say, 'You must not eat from any tree in the garden'?"

The woman said to the serpent, "We may eat fruit from the trees in the garden, but God did say, 'You must not eat fruit from the tree that is in the middle of the garden, and you must not touch it, or you will die.'"

"You will not certainly die," the serpent said to the woman. "For God knows that when you eat from it your eyes will be opened, and you will be like God, knowing good and evil."

When the woman saw that the fruit of the tree was good for food and pleasing to the eye, and also desirable for gaining wisdom, she took some and ate it. She also gave some to her husband, who was with her, and he ate it. Then the eyes of both of them were opened, and they realized they were naked; so they sewed fig leaves together and made coverings for themselves.

Then the man and his wife heard the sound of the Lord God as he was walking in the garden in the cool of the day, and they hid from the Lord God among the trees of the garden. But the Lord God called to the man, "Where are you?"

He answered, "I heard you in the garden, and I was afraid because I was naked; so I hid."

And he said, "Who told you that you were naked? Have you eaten from the tree that I commanded you not to eat from?"

The man said, "The woman you put here with me—she gave me some fruit from the tree, and I ate it."

Then the Lord God said to the woman, "What is this you have done?"

The woman said, "The serpent deceived me, and I ate—"[1]

Poor Eve.

You get blamed for everything.

By your husband.
By history.
By us.

If you hadn't done what you did
we'd never be where we are.

Why did you have to eat the fruit?

And inside our blame is smuggled
a sneering question.
About this God of yours, Eve.
And His one rule.
And that bad bit of fruit.

One rule? We ask, incredulous. One measly bit of fruit?
Please! And the whole world breaks?

What kind of God is that?

And at once we see.
The lie that worked on you, Eve,
works in us still:
"God is not good.
God is not kind.
God does not love you.
If you do what He says, you won't be happy."

Eve, you're not the worst of us.
You're just the first of us.

And we have been sold a bill of goods
with this story we've been told ...

God,
from the very beginning,
You so loved that You gave ...

Before the foundation of the world,
there You are—
Father and Son—
delighting together at the very idea of creating humanity.
At the very idea of human beings.
At the very idea of me.

The word is *frolic*. That's what it says.
Father and Son—both so over the moon
that You are actually frolicking.[2]

What kind of God is this?

∾

In the beginning,
there You are—
down on Your hands and knees
in the mud.
Lifting our face to Yours.
Breathing life into us.
Waking us with a kiss.

What kind of God is this?

As our eyes open—
as we begin to be—
there You are smiling at us.
Teaching us who we are.
Reaching out Your hand to us
giving us Paradise.
Inviting us into the Dance of Joy.

And Love was the ground of our being
and the air in our lungs
and the light in our eyes.
And nothing ever made us afraid. Or sad.

＆

And all You asked of us was love.

To let ourselves be loved by You—
to drink at the fountain of goodness.
To be nurtured and nourished by You.
To increase and multiply.
And by our thriving
praise You.

But You would not demand it. (Love that is not freely given is
not love at all.) So in Your perfect love—as Your gift to us—You
presented us with a tree and a fruit. And the choice.

Would we love You back? Would we choose to trust You—do
what You told us to, simply because we knew You loved us and
could only, ever will our good? Would we choose to believe You
love us?

But rebellion entered the garden. And slithered up to us through
the grasses, whispering a different story in our ears. The slandering
story of a severe, strict, law-obsessed, hard man God. The story of
a punishing, petty, peevish, vengeful, angry joy-killer. The story of
a God who was not to be trusted and did not want our best.

We chose the serpent's story, not Love's.
And it stole away our hearts.
We rose up in mutiny against You, shouting,
"WE WILL BE AS GOD!"

And the ground gave way beneath us
and opened up into hell and pain and death and tears.
And the pain rent the heavens.
And God's heart.

And we lost it all.

One rule? We ask, incredulous. One measly bit of fruit?
Please! And we have to leave Paradise?

What kind of God is that?

But we've been sold a bill of goods
with this story we've been told ...

> *For love is as strong as death....*
> *It burns like blazing fire,*
>   *like a mighty flame.*
> *Many waters cannot quench love;*
>   *rivers cannot sweep it away. (Song 8:6–7)*

Even at the darkest hour,
even as His heart is breaking,
Grace is reaching for us in the dark...

Even as we run from Him and hide in the shadows,
shrinking and afraid
God is moving toward us—calling, "Where are you?"
Not because He doesn't know,
but so we would know.
How far away we are now.
How far He would have to come to find us now.
What a distance He would have to travel to reach us now.

As our shame overwhelms us and we try to cover up with
patched-together fig leaves,
still God is moving toward us.
Not to punish
but protect.
He comes not to scold
but with skins.
Clothes He has made for us,
to cover our shame—
until the day when He would finally bear it all away.

Even in the rubble of His destroyed world,
God is moving toward us.

He is already beginning to seek the lost ...
He is already beginning to rescue the world ...

Our Seeking, Self-Emptying, Coming-After, Rescuing, Self-Giving, Never-Giving-Up, Tenderhearted, Abba Father God!

And then, in His eagerness to bless,
to love,
to save,
—even as He pronounces the sentence of death from sin
(what sin has done, what it will mean now: sickness, tears, death,
and dying)—
He is making a promise ...
"One day I'm going to do battle against the snake. I'll destroy his
work of death and dark and hate and sickness and tears. I'm going
to heal the world! Heaven will be yours again! I'm coming back
for you."

God is telling the Story even angels long to look into,
the Story they never tire of hearing,
the Story they can't stop gazing at in wonder.
The Story of the One Great Love.
And the Great Good News.

> *For God so loved the world that he gave his one and only Son.*
> *(John 3:16)*

And into the darkness, a glimmer of light shines.

To dust you will return now.
Yes, but God once breathed Life into dust ...

There is no way back to Paradise now.
No way to save yourselves.
Yes, but that doesn't mean there is no Way ...

You will suffer now.
Yes, but God is for us.[3]
And one day, will be with us ...[4]

Down the corridors of the centuries, one night, in Bethlehem,
Immanuel will come!

Love Himself
clothed in a man's body.

And, Eve, your name—given to you after the sentence of death—
carries no blame.
Eve—"Mother of Life."
Your name is a promise
telling you the true story of who you are:
It is through you, Eve—not Adam[5]—that Life will come.

Someone will be born into your family, Eve.
He will crush the serpent
and the serpent will strike His heel.
He is the Prince of Life Himself,
born to die—and in dying, to destroy death!

Those thorns on the ground will one day make a crown.

You see, Eve, the first gospel isn't Matthew.
It's Genesis.[6]

And the first person to hear the gospel announced, isn't Mary.
It's you.

Faced with the choice—we reach for the fruit.

We take and eat.

Such small words.
Such an easy act.
So violent the breaking.
So hard the undoing.

God will taste centuries of slander and ridicule and hatred. He
will taste poverty, homelessness, scandalous birth, suffering and
betrayal—and violent death—before He will take those same
words and turn them to our salvation:[7]
"Take and Eat"

And it will heal the whole world.

> *Jesus took bread, and blessed it, and [broke] it, and gave it to the disciples, and said, Take, eat; this is my body. (Matt. 26:26 KJV)*

☙

"WE WILL BE AS GOD!" we cheered in our arrogance.

And in beautiful humility, God says, "I will be as a servant," and steps out of heaven, empties Himself of His Majesty, and comes down.

> *He made himself nothing by taking the very nature of a servant. (Phil. 2:7)*

☙

When we lost Him,
He came to find us.
When we left our place with Him,
He made His place in us.

> *So that Christ may dwell in your hearts through faith. And I pray that you, being rooted and established in love, may have power, together with all the Lord's holy people, to grasp how wide and long and high and deep is the love of Christ, and to know this love that surpasses knowledge—that you may be filled to the measure of all the fullness of God. (Eph. 3:17–19)*

What kind of God is this?

This God of ours!
Whose name is Love!

☙

At the end of time,
Eve, I see you at the Wedding Feast of the Lamb.
When everything sad will come untrue.
When He will wipe every tear from our eyes.
When we will see that there never was a tear shed that was lost.
When we will see how He has woven everything together in this,
His beautiful story of Love, to do such great good to us that we
will hardly be able to take it in ... and only fall on our knees in
adoration.

And as we sit together at His table, Eve,
I hear Him say with tears and great laughter—
"Take
And eat!"

And we do.

L to R: Joy Prouty, Sally Lloyd-Jones,
Leslie Jordan, Amanda Bible Williams

ABOUT THE AUTHOR
Sally Lloyd-Jones

Photo by Bob Boyd

Sally is a *New York Times* bestselling writer and frequent performer of her work. Her books have been critically acclaimed by both the *Wall Street Journal* and the *New York Times* and include *The Jesus Storybook Bible* and *How to Be a Baby*, a *New York Times* Notable Book of the Year.

Sally was born and raised in Africa, schooled in England and at the Sorbonne in Paris, and now lives in New York City. She can be found at www.sallylloyd-jones.com.

"EVEN AT *the darkest* HOUR, EVEN AS *HIS heart* IS BREAKING, GRACE IS *reaching* OUT *for us* IN THE *DARK*."

— *Sally Lloyd-Jones*

Top L to R: Kelly Minter, Sarah Macintosh
Left: Taylor Leonhardt

MARY MAGDALENE

God's Faithfulness in Release

LISTEN ALONG

"A Woman"

"Why are you afraid to forgive him?"

I nervously glanced out the window as my therapist sank into her cozy red chair, crossed her ankles, and waited in silence. The thing I love—and fear—about Shari is how comfortable she is with silence. Maybe she learned to tolerate it in therapy school, like doctors learn to tolerate blood and puke and fluorescent lights in med school. Or maybe she knows our world suffers from noise pollution and just thirty seconds of stillness can clear the air.

It got quieter and quieter, so startlingly still I could feel my pulse in the back of my ears. Avoiding the forgiveness question altogether, I scanned the room and saw Shari's iced green tea on the side table next to her cell phone. To my left, essential oils were diffusing, maybe lemongrass or vetiver. Stacks of books lined shelves on the back wall: Brené Brown's *Daring Greatly* and *The Wounded Heart* by Dan Allender caught my eye.

Ordinarily I would use my cell phone as a "get out of your feelings free" card, scrolling through social media or the news to numb ... but it's sort of an unspoken rule in therapy: no phones allowed unless you're quoting that wild text your friend sent and it's important to get the wording just right. So there I was, invited into holy silence. A beckoning to grow more present to the room, to the moment, to God, and to myself.

I exhaled and closed my eyes, settling into the stillness. Within a minute, my cheeks grew red and the oncoming avalanche in my heart was mirrored by the tears traveling down my face. I cried and cried and cried, sloppily unraveling like a kid rolling down a hill in the middle of summer.

With gentle curiosity, and after approximately one hundred hours of not talking, Shari asked The Question:

"Why are you crying?"

I told her I didn't know. She nodded empathetically. I looked outside again and thought about her first question, the one about forgiveness. I wondered why I clung so tightly to unforgiveness. Why did I feel safe behind a shield of resentment?

You know those old toys and blankets many children cling to for comfort? Growing up, mine was Josefina Montoya, an American Girl doll hailing from New Mexico in 1824. She wore a white blouse with puffy capped sleeves and a beautiful red skirt with southwestern stitching on the bottom. Her braided hair was finished with a touch of yellow primrose. I got her for Christmas when I was six years old. It was the nicest gift I'd ever received. For a few years, Josefina and I were a package deal. She learned about Noah and the flood at Sunday school and read books in my room and ate Lucky Charms with me for breakfast. Then, toward the end of third grade, I looked at Josefina and felt … *different*. Like I had outgrown her.

I was ready for big-girl things like lip gloss and sparkly eyeshadow, not play dolls. I knew it was time to let go of Josefina and, with her, my young childhood.

> *"Forgiving this person meant letting go of other things too. It meant letting go of being a victim."*

Flash forward to middle school, when I saw a segment on *Dr. Phil* about a forty-year-old man who sucked his thumb like a child. My judgmental adolescent brain thought, *What a weirdo!* but in hindsight, he wasn't weird at all. Lots of people hold tightly to quirky coping mechanisms for protection even if they've outgrown them.

Inhaling and exhaling again, I looked Shari in the eyes and tilted my head. I whispered, "Why am I crying?"

I thought of Josefina. I knew unforgiveness was like an old doll I had outgrown, but forgiving this person meant letting go of other things too. It meant letting go of being a victim. Letting go of bitterness toward the church who ignored his abuse. Letting go of the rage that sat dormant at the bottom of my heart like coffee grounds in a Yeti mug. Letting go of entitlement and holding people hostage and privilege. Letting go of control.

I blurted out, "I don't want to let him go because I'm scared of losing my own story in the process!"

She smiled and gently nodded. Solomon said it best:

———

There is a time for everything, and a season for every activity under the heavens." (Eccl. 3:1)

———

There is a time for holding on.

Holding on for dear life because deep inside you know there is something worth living for. Holding on to God's promises when your circumstances are gut wrenching. Holding on to the still voice of Truth when lies from the Enemy feel louder. Holding on to your story when nobody else has ears to listen.

Then there is a time for letting go.

For growing out of old patterns and walking into new ones: patterns driven by abundance instead of scarcity, love instead of fear, and wonder instead of dread. Letting go of bitterness that tastes like honey but acts like poison. Letting go of the right to have *your* life on *your* terms with *your* timing.

It reminds me of a passage in John's gospel.

The story goes that Mary, a friend and disciple of Jesus, visited His burial site three days after He was executed and found the entryway stone rolled away. She peered inside and discovered the tomb was empty except for the linen in which Jesus was buried. Naturally, she created a story in her head to make sense of the situation: *"They have taken the Lord out of the tomb, and we don't know where they have put him" (John 20:2).*

Someone must *have stolen His body!* she thought. *Was it the Romans? The Pharisees? Followers? Merchants? Thieves?* She gathered some disciples to investigate. They saw the tomb and agreed—someone must've taken His body. Maybe disappointed or angry or resigned to their friend's death, everyone but Mary went home.

She stood outside the tomb and cried, mourning the death of her friend, the loss of His body, and a future without His presence in her life. *Things weren't supposed to be this way.*

Just as she settled into the silence, Mary heard The Question:

———

"Woman, why are you crying?..."

Thinking [Jesus] was the gardener, [Mary] said, "Sir, if you have carried him away, tell me where you have put him, and I will get him."

Jesus said to her, "Mary."

She turned toward him and cried out in Aramaic, "Rabboni!" (which means "Teacher").

Jesus said, "Do not hold on to me, for I have not yet ascended to the Father. Go instead to my brothers and tell them, 'I am ascending to my Father and your Father, to my God and your God.'" (vv. 15–17)

———

There it is. The Question.

Why are you crying?

For many years I read this story and projected impatience onto Jesus' tone: "Seriously?! Are you crying *again?* I *told* you I would resurrect. I *told* you I was God! When will you ever learn!" But there's no evidence to suggest Jesus was frustrated with Mary. Instead, I wonder if His tone was a lot like Shari's, marked by curiosity and steadfast love. Maybe His question was less about getting answers and more about exposing the root of Mary's heart.

> *What are you grieving?*
> *Are you disappointed? Angry? Sad?*
> *Why are you afraid of letting go?*

How sacred, messy, and relatable is that moment? She didn't even realize she was talking to Jesus! She was grieving the absence of a person who stood before her, craving the presence of someone just inches away. Yet by clinging to her own version of events ("They've stolen His body!"), she couldn't see the kingdom reality of a resurrected Christ.

Then He said her name, and she knew the truth: *God was with her the entire time.*

Imagine how it would feel to see a man whose execution you witnessed with your own eyes standing before you in the flesh, saying your name. To Mary, it must have felt like a massive clash of competing realities—certain He was dead yet certain He was alive. Convinced of one narrative yet faced with another.

That tension?

That tension is a lot like faith.

It's a flow of letting go, then holding on, then letting go again, leaning on God's voice as your guide. Mary let go of Jesus in His death, feeling all kinds of grief and loss and disappointment. Then, after encountering the resurrected Jesus, she clung to Him with joy! Then Jesus told her, *"Do not hold on to me.... Go instead to my brothers and tell them ..." (v. 17).*

Letting go,

Holding on,

Letting go.

Just like children move from milk to mush to solids, the Christian journey requires similar growth *(Heb. 5:12)*. It necessitates releasing old patterns, rhythms, and systems that *used to work* in order to follow God into greater things.

"Savannah," Shari said, leaning toward me, "do you really think God will leave you out to dry if you choose to let go?"

"No," I replied with a smirk. "But I wish it wasn't such a painful process."

I looked at the clock. My hour was up. I thanked Shari and walked to my car. Closing the door, I noticed something fall out of the passenger side's sun visor and onto the floor. It was a NASA lanyard from years ago when my friend's mom took us on a tour of the Marshall Space Flight Center.

I smiled just thinking about that day. We saw the beginning pieces of a rocket destined for Mars. I remember putting my hand on it and thinking, *I'm touching something that will one day be* on a different planet! We learned about 3D printing machines that hospitals used to create custom prosthetic hands for people. We ate astronaut food and met rocket scientists.

The main thing I remember is a video they played about multistage rockets.

> "It's a flow of letting go, then holding on, then letting go again, leaning on God's voice as your guide."

In (incredibly) oversimplified terms, a multistage rocket is exactly what it sounds like: multiple stages, or rockets, stacked on top of each other. The bottom stage contains fuel for the ground launch and gets the rocket into the air. When the tanks run out of propellant, the first stage detaches from the rocket and falls into the ocean. This propels the second stage into gear, until it runs out of fuel and detaches. This process carries on until only the satellite is in orbit, freed from the dead weight of empty fuel tanks and lower stages.

Sometimes it feels like letting go of the first (or second or third) stage means letting go of the whole rocket, doesn't it? If I let go of that person, will I let go of my story? If I let go of control, will everything fall apart? If I let go of an unhealthy belief about God, am I letting go of God Himself?

This is what a life of faith looks like! Expanding and contracting. Catching and releasing.

Why was I crying? Maybe, just maybe, it was why Mary wept too?

I wonder if that holy silence did a similar work in our hearts. When the dust settled and the disciples went home and Shari leaned back in her red chair and nothing but stillness remained, God's invitation to us rang clear: let go of the way things *should have been* and embrace the way things *are*.

Maybe you feel this way? Like you're clinging tightly to something you've outgrown but you're not sure who you'd be without it? Maybe it's coping with food. Maybe it's shame. Maybe it's unforgiveness. Maybe you fill your schedule to the brim in order to escape the stillness.

Maybe it's codependency or addiction or victimhood. Maybe it's so intertwined in your story it feels impossible to break free.

What would it look like for you to slow down and accept God's invitation into silence? What would it look like to feel the grief around a childhood wound? To feel the weight of disappointment around your story, life, marriage, or career?

Do you believe God is faithful to meet you there?

In the same way God met Mary two thousand years ago near an empty tomb, God met me in my therapist's office in 2019, and God will meet you in your car or the grocery store or your kitchen or closet. There is no fear in unclenching your hands in release, because God will never let go of you. There will be moments you're faced with two competing realities: one bent toward control and safety, the other toward vulnerability and faith. Look to Mary's example and choose faith. Let go of the old and cling to the new. *"Lean not on your own understanding" (Prov. 3:5)* but on the goodness of God.

Know this: God doesn't do failed rocket launches. He works in stages. He works to propel you. He works to free you. He is empathetic toward you. He knows it can be scary to let go of the thing that launched you from the ground into the air! He understands how often you'd rather hold on to dead weight because you're used to it and it's comfortable. But His intention for you is to propel you further than you imagined. Upward in faith, onward in love.

Father, I trust that You are good and Your intentions are kind. Please show me anything I'm clinging to that stands in the way of fully trusting You. I don't want to hide behind control, resentment, or fear. I want to let go and live a life of faith. My heart is Yours. I trust Your process and I trust Your ways.

Amen.

ABOUT THE AUTHOR
Savannah Locke

Photo by Jayda Iye

Savannah is a writer from Franklin, Tennessee. She is wife to Todd and (dog) mom to Bentley.

"THERE IS *no fear* IN *UNCLENCHING your* HANDS *IN RELEASE* BECAUSE GOD WILL *never let go* OF YOU."

— *Savannah Locke*

Amanda Bible Williams

NAOMI

God's Faithfulness in Tragedy

Dark, thunderous clouds fill the sky. Even the slightest glimpse of sunshine is quenched by the cumulonimbus.

You take a step of faith and walk outside. Big balls of frozen ice begin to fall, hitting you one by one. It hurts. It doesn't make sense.

Keep walking …

The dark clouds seem to close in around you. Each step is harder and more treacherous.

Keep walking …

The farther you walk, the harder it gets. "This plodding is so rot with pain," you mumble as you look ahead.

There in the distance is a ray of sunlight. You remember that beautiful inheritance. You know it's coming.

Keep walking …

It's an act of valiant faith to put one foot in front of the other.

Keep walking …

You're going to make it to the end. Weak. Tired. But hopeful, because of that little ray, that faint but sure ray.

Keep walking …

And when you get there, you'll realize He has always been there.[1]

I have experienced those dark clouds. It's a familiar scene. Loss is something I'm all too familiar with: my father died when I was nineteen years old, I lost four children to miscarriage, and my oldest sister passed away at age forty. Even now, listing it out can feel overwhelming. During seasons of discouragement, loss, or confusion, you and I go searching for answers or even the slightest glimmer of hope. That's one of the many reasons I'm so thankful for God's Word. God was gracious to tell the stories of those who have gone before us, who, like many of us, experienced times when everything seemed to be surrounded by dark clouds.

"I have experienced those dark clouds. It's a familiar scene."

In the book of Ruth, we find such a story.

Famine, loss of homeland, loss of husband, and loss of children. They're something no one would ever wish for. We see all these great losses in Naomi's life in the book of Ruth. So often we look at these passages and only glance over Naomi. We admire the loyalty of Ruth in staying with her mourning mother-in-law. We also look to the love story of Boaz and Ruth as proof that Mr. Right could come from any circumstance if we display enough trust. And, rightly, we see the faithfulness of God within dire circumstances. But if we focus on Naomi, we see that she faced great tragedy and feared that only more would come. But as is the case so often, God provided far above all that she imagined.

NAOMI'S FEAR OF TRAGEDY

Naomi wholeheartedly believed that the Lord had dealt bitterly with her. Twice we see this referenced in the first chapter. First, she urged her daughters-in-law to leave her. She said she desired that they be cared for and that they find new husbands. She knew she was too old to conceive more sons, and if she did, the women would have to wait until the sons were grown to remarry. (Not to mention that Naomi herself would have to find a new husband, since hers had died as well.) All these factors coming together were inconceivable to Naomi, so she urged the women to leave, adding, *"No, my daughters. It is more bitter for me than for you, because the LORD's hand has turned against me!" (Ruth 1:13).*

She did not desire any further tragedy for her daughters. The women wept. As we know, one left. However, Ruth stayed.

Next, we see that Naomi and Ruth traveled to Bethlehem (where Naomi was from). When they encountered the women who lived there, they asked if it was indeed Naomi. She responded:

———

Don't call me Naomi," she told them. "Call me Mara, because the Almighty has made my life very bitter. I went away full, but the LORD has brought me back empty. Why call me Naomi? The LORD has afflicted me; the Almighty has brought misfortune upon me." (vv. 20–21)

———

Naomi not only believed the Lord was angry with her, she urged the women to call her Mara, a name she chose because it reflected how she saw her new identity: bitter *(Ex. 15:23)*. Only because we're familiar with the end of the story do we know that Naomi misinterpreted her circumstances and applied wrath where there was none.

Some of us, perhaps like Naomi, think God is out to get us, and so we wait for the next tragedy, assuming the worst about Him. We'd never say it, but we can tend to exercise our faith in a way that communicates we're convinced God is tyrannical. God is not tyrannical. He is loving. He can't do anything contrary to His love for us. Even hard circumstances turn out for our good *(Rom. 8:28)*. You and I can rest in the assurance of His love.

Despite her sorrow, Naomi loved Ruth and desired good for her. To make a short story even shorter, Naomi coached Ruth and instructed her on how to win over Boaz. Ruth obeyed, married Boaz, and bore a son. What is beautiful is how the same women that Naomi told to call her Mara are the women at the end of the story who point Naomi to the faithfulness of God:

The women said to Naomi: "Praise be to the LORD, who this day has not left you without a guardian-redeemer. May he become famous throughout Israel! He will renew your life and sustain you in your old age. For your daughter-in-law, who loves you and who is better to you than seven sons, has given him birth." (Ruth 4:14–15)

We can learn a great deal here. First, consider if Naomi had hidden all her fear and bitterness. What if, instead of being open and honest and raw, she had chosen to put on a good face and share platitudes? Her honesty allowed for others to minister to her. They reminded her of the love and faithfulness of God to her. You and I can often share that quip "I'm fine"

when we are not, even when speaking to our closest friends. The Lord used Naomi's vulnerability to point us back to Him and show us all that He was doing in her life. He so often does the same for us. When we are open and honest, our real needs become known and we can then look back and see the faithfulness, restoration, and goodness of the Lord.

"Even hard circumstances turn out for our good. You and I can rest in the assurance of His love."

Oh, the great faithfulness of God—as much to Naomi as to Ruth. In the Lord's faithfulness to Naomi, through her daughter-in-law Ruth, He provided far and above all that she could have requested. And we know that God carried out a great redemption plan through this story as well. Ruth and Boaz's son, Obed, was the father of

Jesse, and Jesse the father of David, which eventually led to the Messiah's birth *(Rom. 15:12)*.

> *"I can affirm that a great deal of my learning to trust the Lord for my future— clinging to my Savior—has come through sorrows."*

Many of us don't actually go through tragedy as much as we fear the potential for tragedy. I have struggled with a fear of the future, waiting for the worst to happen. I fear that danger is right around the corner. As I shared at the beginning, I've tasted enough tragedy to know that life is hard and pain often is just around the corner. In many ways, perhaps, I've always been in a state of waiting for the next hard thing. I don't mean that to sound melancholy or pessimistic. On the contrary, I'm hopeful!

The Lord has always been near to me throughout my trials. I've experienced His faithfulness and His steadfast love. Paul tells us that suffering produces endurance *(Rom. 5:3)*. I can affirm that a great deal of my learning to trust the Lord for my future— clinging to my Savior—has come through sorrows. Paul concludes this text by reminding us that our hope will not put us to shame *(v. 5)*.

But we live in a Genesis 3 world, where the curse affects every aspect of our lives. Death and tragedy happen every single day. While some are close enough that we experience them, most are outside our narrow view. But like Naomi, we are not walking alone. God is with us and for us; He is on our side *(Rom. 8:31)*.

You and I can resist the temptation to fear by remembering the character and nature of our Lord—and the promises of His Word. *Isaiah 41:10* records God's declaration to us:

———

> *Fear not, for I am with you; be not dismayed, for I am your God; I will strengthen you, I will help you, I will uphold you with my righteous right hand. (ESV)*

———

God is our God. He is holy—set apart—and yet He is personal. He told us we would experience suffering *(John 16:33)*, but we also have the promise that He will be with us *(2 Cor. 1:3)*—and with all Christians throughout the world.

Even if terror prevails for a time on this earth, the truth of His great care for us will not wane. In the midst of fearful things, He promises to be our strength. He promises to help you and me and to hold onto us with His righteous right hand. We serve a faithful and loving God who will not desert us.

If we've placed our faith and trust in Jesus, you and I can say with great relief: "We can do nothing apart from Jesus—even trust is dependent on His grace." That seems like an odd statement, I know. You may wonder, *Why in the world is that a relief?*

Because we aren't calling on a weak, uncaring, aloof god. It's a relief to remember the character of the One we call on and that we can do nothing apart from Him *(John 15:5)*. God gives us the grace we need to cast our fears onto Him. We can rest assured the Lord will continue to work mightily, even when, like Naomi, we can't see it.

Let this story build your faith. We don't see all that God sees, and we don't know all that God knows. We only see in part—*"We walk by faith, not by sight"* *(2 Cor. 5:7 esv)*. So we cling to that glimmer of hope and run to His throne of grace. If you are facing a tough circumstance, pray that God would give you fresh faith to walk, though blindly, with trust in Him, knowing that He has laid out your path. And like Naomi, each of our paths ultimately leads to our Messiah.

Lord, You are awesome and mighty. You are holy and good. You are the great I AM. You gave Your Son Jesus for us so we might approach Your throne of grace. It is for this reason we come before You and ask for mercy for our communities and the world.

Amen.

ABOUT THE AUTHOR
Trillia Newbell

Trillia Newbell is the author of several books including *Sacred Endurance, If God Is for Us, Fear and Faith,* and the kids' book *God's Very Good Idea.* You can find her at trillianewbell.com.

"*GOD* GIVES US *the grace* WE *NEED* TO CAST *our fears* ONTO HIM."

— *Trillia Newbell*

Top L to R: Ruth Chou Simons, Ellie Holcomb, Raechel Myers
Right L to R: Lisa Harper, Raechel Myers, Trillia Newbell

Faithful

ESTHER

God's Faithfulness to Us Nobodies

Selfless love is surprising—even confusing. When I think back on the big and small moments in my life when I was the recipient of confounding kindness, I confess I still scratch my head at my undeserved favor.

A couple of years ago, while my sister was helping her kids pack for summer camp, she found an old MP3 player in her attic. It didn't even have a screen, and at its prime, it held only eleven songs. She was fourteen when she first received it, and it's important to me that you know that one of those eleven songs was "Mah Nà Mah Nà" from *The Muppet Show.* So to all the people who thought my big sister looked cool listening to her headphones that year (I sure thought she did), she was secretly just humming "doot doo de doo doo" along with fuzzy puppets.

She showed the clunky silver square to me after she found it, and we reminisced about what a thoughtful and kind early-nineties Christmas gift this was to receive from our stepmom. Her love didn't make sense to us; we weren't her daughters. "I wonder why she took such care with us," I asked. "Do you think she felt like she had to? Was she trying to impress our dad? What was she trying to achieve with all those gifts?" My husband overheard our conversation and laughed. "Babe, have you ever considered that she just truly loved you?" We honestly had not.

When I was a young wife and still in college, money was extremely tight. Like "ramen for dinner every night, but on special occasions we'd add a few sugar snap peas for a treat" tight. In that season, a woman from our church loved me in a way that didn't make sense to me. Marianne was only about fifteen years older than me, and her family was on a budget too. But she would occasionally leave bags of

> *"I was the recipient of confounding kindness; I confess I still scratch my head at my undeserved favor."*

groceries outside our apartment door for us to find, and she and her husband would invite us over for meals—which included meat! She and I once spent an afternoon browsing our favorite secondhand store together—just for fun. The next day the fifteen-dollar purse I was so taken by was waiting for me in our apartment hallway along with a kind note. Why did she do this for me? Any of it? There were lots of college girls at that church, and I wasn't the most interesting one by a long shot. She just chose me and loved me. I still don't know why.

> "*Scripture is full of examples of regular folks being called into unbelievable responsibility and blessing.*"

When I was a kid, our family wasn't able to take vacations. But because my aunt and uncle always included me in their family trips, I enjoyed the mist from Niagara Falls and spent most of my adolescent summers swimming on the rocky beaches in Maine. It was the Merki family, plus Raechel. They made me one of them. They didn't have to invite me; they had three kids of their own. I was known for eating a lot of licorice, and I introduced their children to dc Talk, so it certainly was a risk to take me along. But for a week or two each summer, I got a peek into a family with a mom and a dad. I still remember watching how my aunt and uncle loved each other and related to their children. It became an important reference point for me later when Ryan and I had our own children.

I don't know why these people chose to love me and treat me with such illogical kindness. I realize it's funny that we are tempted to look for deeper meanings and ulterior motives in love. Our own hearts are often so jaded that instances of faithful love and selfless favor can confuse us, even make us skeptical.

Here's the thing: I'm a simple girl from a small town in Michigan. I have social anxiety and I'm a mediocre conversationalist. I don't understand the rules of football or what exactly a key change is. I'm not tall; I have my Belgian grandfather's nose and my German great-grandmother's ankles. I had a complicated childhood and I don't trust people easily. And did I mention the ankles? I don't merit trips to Paris and ice cream sundaes, and I don't deserve manicures and swimming pools.

Yes, I'm wildly special simply because God created me in His image. There isn't a single thing about me that makes me any more important than anyone else. I certainly haven't earned the favor I enjoy in the eyes of those around me. It is God who makes somebodies out of every one of us nobodies.

∽

Isn't it tempting—and risky—to look at someone and assess their importance based on what you see? Scripture is full of examples of regular folks being called into unbelievable responsibility and blessing. Only a few people in Scripture were born into positions of holy influence, but there are hundreds of men and women like Rahab, Moses, Mary, and the boy who offered his fish and loaves to Jesus. These were just ordinary people who served an extraordinary God. That's us too! God's story is full of a vast cloud of witnesses comprised of regular people like me, you, and my friend Marianne. God does some of His best work with us nobodies.

If I had to decide, I'd say my favorite biblical nobody is Esther. Scripture tells us that while she did have a lovely appearance (no Belgian noses in her lineage!), she had no fortune and very little family. She was just an orphan with a kind cousin. But God's favor made her a somebody. And that somebody had the privilege of being used by God to save the Jewish people from destruction.

There is a word for this covenantal favor, this unmerited belonging, this loving-kindness, this loyal love, but it's not an English one. It is the Hebrew word *hesed*. It's an immensely complex word because it is used to describe something that only comes from God Himself. Some scholars help us understand it by explaining that, in most cases, the secular or human version of *hesed* is simply the word *favor*. But there is a significant difference.

Favor is a popular word in the book of Esther. It's used eight times in ten chapters and becomes a theme of our beautiful nobody's story. While it's mostly used to describe relationships between humans (and is mostly a result of Esther's beauty), it's used twice to describe God's actions toward Esther (nothing to do with her outward appearance).

Esther found the favor of King Ahasuerus[1] and his servants because she was lovely. But she found favor with Yahweh because He is lovely. Do you see how *hesed* is so much more complex and meaningful than *favor*?

Michael Card, in his in-depth work *Inexpressible*, defines the *hesed* of God like this: "When the person from whom I have a right to expect nothing gives me everything."[2] Goodness, isn't this a beautiful idea? I've been talking about the favor I've received from family and friends, and I suppose one could assume that I actually would be right to expect a little bit of kindness from them. But what about from those I've hurt? What about from the God I've sinned against again and again? He doesn't owe me anything at all. In fact, I am in actual debt to Him. God's favor isn't our hard-earned right. His *hesed* is the overflowing of His deep covenantal love for us. And His *hesed* was extended not only to Esther but to all Jewish people.

When we belong to God, His *hesed* belongs to us. We can work our tails off to attract the favor of the world, but what if, instead, we rested in the unearned, already-ours favor of the King of Kings?

∽

Sometimes God shows His kind of favor by turning circumstances on their heads. Have you ever seen something that looks like a total loss turn out to have some real nice bits after all or even end up being the key to something new and wonderful? My best friend met her husband because she got a rejection letter from her top college pick. I ended up winning a design prize because I had terrible poison ivy that forced me to stay home and give all my attention to the task. Esther's story is a fascinating series of reversals—instances when God shows favor and faithfulness in surprising ways.

The philosopher Aristotle called this reversal of fortunes *peripety*.[3] According to him, it is the most powerful part of a story. And he's right—we see it in good stories all the time. It's the moment that comes out of the blue and totally changes everything but also feels so right, like it was supposed to happen all along. Shakespeare's works are full of lovers who start off hating each other, have a moment of realization, and fall in love like we knew they should.

We sometimes call it the "twist" in a movie. And I love a movie with a twist (as long as it's not too scary or too long or too dark and there are pretty dresses and great lipstick). One of my favorite movies is *Ocean's Eleven* (the new one, not the old one). If you haven't watched it yet, I am going to spoil it for you, so put your hands over your eyes if you need to. The crew schemes to rob a casino, and they rehearse an elaborate eleven-man plan to execute the heist. At the crucial moment, decoy bags of money are used to clear the way for the team to return disguised as SWAT and steal the money that was already supposed to have been stolen. When it looks like their plan has completely failed, it has actually clicked into gear and they get away with $150 million. At this point, you've bonded with the characters, and they are stealing from a "bad" man, so you suddenly find yourself on your feet cheering for felons to succeed. It is a complete and surprise reversal of their fortunes.

> *"Our own salvation is as staggering a reversal of fortune as can be imagined."*

And do you remember the film *Titanic*? A spoiler here too: the ship does sink. In the beginning of the film, wealthy Rose DeWitt Bukater falls in love with the penniless Jack Dawson. Unfortunately for the fictional young loves, and also for the actual people aboard this mighty ship, the *Titanic* sinks and they are thrown into the North Sea. Rose chooses to stay with Jack instead of boarding one of the limited lifeboats. They drift in the frozen waters, Rose atop a makeshift

raft and Jack holding on to its side, until the cold overtakes him and he dies. This, of course, left us all thinking, *Why didn't Rose just scoot over on the raft! There was room for both of them, and Jack could have been saved!* Nonetheless, after she is rescued alone, Rose sheds the wealth and protection of her family and chooses instead to take Jack's name and make her own way. She boards the *Titanic* as an unhappy, pampered woman but comes to shore as one who has loved and lost (expensive blue necklace notwithstanding).

We love to see these dramatic reversals in stories, and we long to see them in actual lives. Our own salvation is as staggering a reversal of fortune as can be imagined. The book of Esther is a uniquely dense catalog of God's perfect providence in seven surprising and satisfying reversals. Powerless people rescued from evil rulers. The lowly delivered from wicked plans. No one in this book boasted in his own glory without being humbled. Yet, the humble were exalted. It's really pretty wild—take a look.

First, consider the two faces of King Ahasuerus. He was introduced as powerful, extravagant, merry, and pompous—I wouldn't want to go to his party either *(Esther 1:1–8)*. But right after all his self-conscious showmanship, the king was embarrassed and angered when Vashti, his queen, did not come when called *(v. 12)*. His brave face was actually pretty fragile.

Second, the two queens—Vashti and Esther. While we know Vashti refused to come when summoned, this is almost all we know about her: she was the queen who said no. Then Esther (who was *not invited*) did later appear before the king, which was unprecedented *(8:3–4)*. Esther is the queen who said yes, but her yes was spoken to God first.

The third (pretty staggering) reversal is that of Esther's place in the world. She was introduced to us as an orphan, under the care of her cousin Mordecai *(2:5–7)*. Her prospects weren't bright. But she ascended to become the queen of all Persia *(vv. 15–18)*. Esther didn't just slide into queenship and keep quiet, hoping not to risk her neck. She was able to use her position to save her people—God's people.

Fourth is the satisfying change in the fate of cousin Mordecai. Even though Mordecai was a hero who rendered great service to the king, Haman devised a plan to execute him *(3:2–5; 5:14)*. But one night, when the king couldn't sleep, he called for the history books to be opened (a sure cure for sleeplessness). He remembered that although Mordecai had saved his life, he had never rewarded him. Ahasuerus turned everything around and honored Mordecai instead of

allowing him to be executed—in the literal nick of time *(6:10)*.

The looming gallows built by Haman are the fifth dramatic reversal in the book of Esther (and my particular favorite). Haman erected them as tall as he could and planned to hang Mordecai for all the city to see *(5:9–14)*. But in a real "hoisted by his own petard" moment, the king instead had Haman hanged for his treachery on the very gallows he built to torment and kill Mordecai *(7:10)*. So stinking satisfying.

> *"Esther didn't just slide into queenship and keep quiet, hoping not to risk her neck."*

The act of bowing down is the sixth reversal. Early in the story, Haman demanded that Mordecai bow before him in worship *(3:1–2)*. But at the end of his life, instead of subjugating others, Haman actually bowed before Esther, pleading for mercy *(7:7–8)*. Instead of being remembered as a strong Persian hero, Haman has been laughed at and mocked for thousands of years. To this day he is the butt of jokes, and Haman-hat-shaped cookies are baked during the Feast of Purim to celebrate his undoing.

Which leads to the final reversal. Haman set out to annihilate the entire Jewish population in Persia *(3:8–11)*. But after Haman was put to death, the king established a Jewish festival and gave Haman's house to Esther——and Mordecai moved into the house of the very man who hated them and their God. The God of Israel was worshipped—and right under his former roof *(8:1–2)*. Can you think of a better ending than this?

When it was all said and done, King Ahasuerus and Mordecai established a Jewish festival that would have infuriated Haman. Even the name mocks him and celebrates all the peripety of the story. This festival is called Purim, and it comes from the word *pur*, which means "lots" or "dice" (named for the lots cast by Haman to determine the day of the Jewish slaughter). This two-day festival of joy and celebration pauses life to cele-brate God's providential faithfulness and unfailing love—His *hesed*. What Haman put to chance, God worked in His own good providence. It's like Joseph's words to his brothers at the end of Genesis: *"You meant evil against me,*

but God meant it for good" (Gen. 50:20 ESV). Even the Devil and all his scheming belong to God.

∾

The *hesed* of God is demonstrated powerfully in all of Scripture, but I am especially grateful for the particular look at His covenant loyalty in the story of Esther. If you've read Esther, you may have noticed that the name of God is never mentioned—not once. Even still, the book demonstrates a clear theology of divine faithfulness. God made a promise to continue the line of Abraham's descendants way back in Genesis 15, and His loyalty to that promise drives and defines the narrative without mention of His name.

Behind the specifics of her story is the greater context of Esther. Like Esther, all Israel was orphaned and exiled, no longer living in their own homeland but eating from someone else's table. The *hesed* of the never-mentioned but ever-present God intrudes again and again in the narrative. All the essential events in the story happen with passive human characters. How does Esther come before the king? It seems impossible. How does she find favor? Gorgeous eyes only get you so far. How is Mordecai always in the right place at the right time? Seriously, how? Who is actually moving the overturning of men and nations and rescuing a destitute people?

All these things are God's loving-kindness, His *hesed*.

When we see even a glimpse of what He is doing (and that's usually all we get), in contrast to just how undeserving we are, it produces gratefulness and humility in us. God's *hesed* becomes a gentle rebuke to every worry and fear, to every self-driven and self-focused effort. It is a reminder that all we have and all we are we have received from His hands.

Favor calls us to effort, but *hesed* beckons us to rest.

Favor insists that we try, while *hesed* reminds us to trust.

Favor is about what we are, but *hesed* is about who He is.

Like the Jews in Susa, we are somebodies who have been handed back our lives, and the favor of the King on top of it. And the proper response is not a Haman-handed grasping but a thankful return of the kindness we have received. The proper response is thanksgiving, with great joy. *"We love because he first loved us" (1 John 4:19).*

One more reversal: our feasting looks different too. We leave behind the feast at the beginning of the story, glutted with debauchery and self-celebration. Instead, we feast and invite others to join us in a banquet of praise. We give generous gifts and groceries and belonging with an open hand to one another because we have received everything as a gift ourselves. We respond by living our lives as a festival in celebration of the peripety of our salvation, and of the loving-kindness, the favor, the *hesed* of God.

Top L to R: Jess Ray, Amanda Bible Williams
Bottom: Savannah Locke

God of Esther, God of Mordecai, God of Abraham, You kept Your promise to make a people for Yourself, and through Your Son You have invited me into that heritage and all those promises. Help me to find rest in Your loyal loving-kindness. And help me to live a life in response to the salvation that I cannot earn—an openhanded celebration of Your *hesed* toward me. Let my every step, every breath, every moment be those of a woman who has the unearned but unwavering favor of the King of Kings.

Amen.

ABOUT THE AUTHOR
Raechel Myers

Raechel Myers is the cofounder and CEO of She Reads Truth. She lives her life in grateful response to the beauty, goodness, and truth in Scripture and the world. Raechel lives in Nashville with her husband and kids. She loves to travel, cook, eat delicious food, and meander through art galleries.

"IT IS GOD *who makes* SOMEBODIES OUT *of EVERY* ONE OF US *nobodies*."

— *Raechel Myers*

Standing: Ruth Chou Simons
Seated L to R: Ellie Holcomb, Nathan Nockels, Christy Nockels,
Ginny Owens, Trillia Newbell, Lisa Harper

MIRIAM

God's Faithfulness in the Middle of the Story

When I meet a woman who tells me how to faithfully live between a rock and a hard place, there's no way I can know that three days later will turn out to be one of the most crushing days of my life.

At the side of a crowded room, she tells me in quiet tones that her marriage was fighting hard to survive a crisis—when she found herself unexpectedly expecting. In the middle of not knowing how to breathe through all the unknown, she made the choice to fight for joy, to fight for hope, to write down one thousand gifts she was thankful for by picking up a pen and wielding it like a sword—grace upon grace, giving thanks for one small thing at a time. When she held her surprise babe in arms, she named her Grace. She tells me she was holding twenty-seven-day-old baby Grace when this brand-new baby girl unexpectedly seized. Her cherished baby Grace was diagnosed with a brain bleed that left her blind.

In the back of her head, an evil hissed, *So you thought you were being faithful, but look at your life now. Is this grace, all this unexpected, that's left you in this place? Is this all actually grace?*

But the woman didn't waver. She tells me how in the ICU she held her baby girl's hand with one hand and a pen with the other and defiantly and faithfully continued to count her blessings, because she believed it, and I witnessed it in her eyes: faith gives thanks in the middle of the story. Faith sees how there is much to give thanks for now, which gives much hope for the future. The same faithful God who is giving grace upon grace now will faithfully come to meet us in the future with grace upon grace.

> *"Faith sees how there is much to give thanks for now, which gives much hope for the future."*

"You know how you are living through this crisis right now?" asks her trauma therapist while sitting across from this brave mama after she explains her daily, faithful practice of counting gifts and giving thanks. "You are literally finding the strength to live through this crisis—because you have. Just like one creates a memory muscle, you have created a gratitude muscle."

In the middle of her crisis, this woman was already in the middle of strengthening her gratitude muscle—*which was giving her strength.*

I memorize what I read in the woman's eyes:

To stay strong in crisis, you have to exercise your gratitude muscle.

A memory muscle results from working and practicing a motion so your body remembers what to do.

When you faithfully practice your *gratitude muscle*, your soul remembers *what to do in crisis.*

When you daily work out your *gratitude muscle*, even in crisis, your soul daily remembers how to move toward joy.

Exercise your *gratitude muscle*— to grow strong in joy.

This is what I want to tell this woman who faithfully works out her gratitude muscle to grow strong in joy and certain in hope: *you are a woman with a Miriam Mind.*

Open up the Greatest Story and read the Exodus event—this great Way out of a nightmarish crisis—and you see how *Miriam was a woman who had every reason to grow bitter but she rebelled against hopelessness.* Miriam's very name embodied who she was, her name having two meanings. First, *Miriam* comes from the Hebrew root *mar*, which means "bitterness." That is exactly what the Egyptians intended for Miriam and her people: *"They [the Egyptians] embittered ['vayemareru,'*

from the root 'mar'] their life with hard labour" (Ex. 1:14).[1]

Bitterness was what the Israelites were eating in Egypt— slaves enslaved to bitterness. Under the taskmaster's whip, hope can be beaten to a pulp. You know that whip: the whip of hard times, the whip of brutal relationships, the whip of stinging losses. When life doesn't seem fair, bitterness can become your daily fare. Miriam's earliest formation was by the bitterness of annihilation and national decimation—and yet she hoped beyond hope. She God-hoped beyond grasping-hope—for a faithful-hope.

While one meaning of her name means "bitterness," Miriam also embodied the second meaning of her name—"rebellion"—from the root *meri.* There were Israelite slave women who also were actual *rebels against hopelessness.* Though their male babies were being killed, it was the women who continued to turn to their exhausted husbands, the men who were being whipped, beaten, and driven relentlessly, because these faithful women desired (even in these circumstances) to conceive more babies. Though Pharaoh was trying to destroy the future of the people of Israel by the systematic slaughter of one male baby at a time, it was the faithful women who continued to bear children in defiant hope for the continuation of the nation of Israel *(vv. 19–21)*.

There was a whole tribe of women who were faithful rebels against hopelessness.

Though their neighbors were calling out for their death and oppression, the women were calling to their people, "You cannot afford to lose hope. No one can make us a slave to hopelessness. At all costs—for the sake of your life: You have to be a rebel against hopelessness. And hope in God."

In the midst of the hellish crisis of the death and genocide of their families, when Moses's mother *"could no longer hide him, she took a box made of reeds for him, and ... put the child in it, and laid it in the reeds by the river's bank. His sister [Miriam] stood far off, to see what would be done to him"* (2:3–4 NHEB).

With her brother in a basket of reeds, Miriam was standing in a current of streaming water, and she was waiting.

A woman with a Miriam Mind, she waits not to see if God will move but how God will move.

In the thicket of bushes, Miriam knew what God's people have always known: God always provides grace upon grace; God always provides a ram in the thicket; God always provides hope in the most intense crisis.

Miriam stood at the edge of the water and witnessed Batyah,[2] the daughter of Pharaoh, come to bathe in the Nile River, come to hear the cries of Moses, much like God heard the cries of His people. Miriam watched Batyah rescue the child that Batyah's own father, the pharaoh, decreed to die. Miriam bravely approached the daughter of the most powerful man in the land and offered to bring a Hebrew woman to nurse the baby—the baby's own mother. And our faithful Father had Moses rescued from the waters and raised by his own mother to know His redemptive ways *(2:5–9)*.

Even when it feels like all hope is lost, Hope never stops coming to find you.

Several decades later, when the people of God stood on the shores of what we've translated as the Red Sea— but is actually the Reed Sea—the people of God quaked with terror to see the Egyptian army barreling down upon them. But Moses and Miriam, sister and brother (whom God rescued out of a basket of reeds), led the people to trust the faithfulness of their God, who split that Reed Sea so His people could walk through impossible waves and out onto dry land.

This is what God always does: *a bruised reed He will not break, but He will break open whatever Reed Sea you face.*

On the other side of the Reed Sea, broken open by God to make a way where there seemed to be no way,

Moses sang what Jews to this day call the Song of the Sea, the Shirat HaYam:

———

I will sing to the LORD,
for he is highly exalted....
The LORD is my strength and
my defense;
he has become my salvation....
Who is like you—
majestic in holiness,
awesome in glory,
working wonders?
(Exodus 15:1–2, 11)

———

But Miriam's brother Moses wasn't the only one who sang. The Jewish Talmud states, "There were three excellent leaders for Israel. They were Moses, Aaron, and Miriam." While Moses and Aaron were leaders for all the people, "Miriam was the teacher of the women."[3] Like Sarah, a mother of nations of whom God says, *"I will bless her,... and she will be a mother of nations"* (Gen. 17:16 NHEB), Miriam too was one of the faith mothers, one of the church mothers. Like Sarah before her, and Deborah, Hannah, Abigail, Esther, and Huldah after her, Miriam too was noted in God's Book as one of the prophetesses who faithfully led the people of God, serving and teaching

and leading and guiding. Like all the prophetesses of God, Miriam did not change the Word or twist the Word or minimize the Word or water down the Word but was a faithful woman of God who served up the Word of God fearlessly and faithfully to the people of God.

The people of God have always needed leaders who are the faith mothers.

One of those direly needed faith mothers standing there on the other side of the Reed Sea was Miriam.

———

Miriam the prophetess, the sister of Aaron, took a tambourine in her hand; and all the women went out after her with tambourines and with dances. Miriam answered them, "Sing to the LORD." (Ex. 15:20–21 NHEB).

———

When the Jewish women left Egypt with their families, they had to leave so hastily that they were not even able to finish baking their bread but instead carried it on their backs, letting the bread bake as matzah simply from the heat of their backs. Though the Jewish women had little time to prepare food, they ensured they made time to grab their tambourines.

Because thanksgiving to God is what feeds a soul with joy in God. Because thanksgiving grows us strong in God.

> # *"When you faithfully practice your gratitude muscle day in and day out, your soul remembers what to do in crisis."*

Because that's what you do in a crisis when you have a gratitude muscle: you reach for your tambourine. When a situation feels out of control, you have to reach out for an instrument to give thanks to the One who is in control. *When you faithfully practice your gratitude muscle day in and day out, your soul remembers what to do in crisis.* When you practice gratitude every day, you'll find that someday when you're in an impossible place, your soul will remember how to give thanks, so that joy is always, always, always possible for you, even in that place.

In the middle of the night, in the middle of the crisis, Miriam, a leader of women and a faith mother, taught her women to have a Miriam Mind: *the most important way to prepare for a crisis is to be prepared to give thanks.*

Instead of complaints at the ready—have your tambourine at the ready. Instead of being quick to give in to despair—always be quick to give thanks to God. Instead of being overwhelmed—be ready to flex your trained gratitude muscle because of your deeply ingrained trust in the One who overcomes.

Every Faithful Rebel against hopelessness knows it: *one of your greatest weapons against hopelessness—is gratefulness.*

Faith gives thanks in the middle of the story because, essentially, what is essential is that you have your tambourine always ready, that the timbre of your heart is always a song of thanks to God.

I'm profoundly mesmerized by this woman with a Miriam Mind standing in front of me, boldly smiling as she shows me photos of her little girl, Grace, now. Grace beaming and thriving and flourishing in her own exquisitely beautiful way. This faith mother is a Faithful Rebel against hopelessness who warriors through every crisis with gratefulness.

As she reaches over to hug me, I'm held with the truth: *hold on to your tambourine so you can hold on to hope.*

Hold on to your instrument of thanksgiving so you can hold on to what's life giving.

Never lose your thanksgiving tambourine—so you never lose hope.

I had no idea how I would need a Miriam Mind, to grow my gratitude muscle, when our own family crisis tsunamied us three days later.

> "*Grace beaming and thriving and flourishing in her own exquisitely beautiful way.*"

But I had my tambourines ready—three of them. A collection of tambourines, hanging on a wall right near the kitchen sink so I could see them at every turn. So I could be a Miriam.

I soak dishes and my heart leaks, but those tambourines of our faith mother, Miriam, they stir in me a song of thanks anyway—a gratefulness that defiantly rises from a life of faithfulness. And I flex my faith with thanks for grace upon grace and feel this gratitude muscle growing stronger, my own heart beating louder with a thankfulness that gives way to hopefulness.

In between a rock and a hard place, there's this irresistible invitation to be a Faithful Rebel against the bitter dark, to trust enough to sing the Song of the Sea:

Sing, heart, sing your thanks,
Grow your gratitude muscle,
Grow in thanks to God, grow
    strong in God
and trust there is no calamity,
agony, enemy, or catastrophe
that can change this certainty:

Mercy meets you
and Grace names you
and Hope holds you
and Courage carries you
and the King of Kings claims you
so no past can ever shame you,
no scar can ever maim you,
no choice can ever stain you,
more than His love faithfully
    sustains you.

Women with a Miriam Mind of thankfulness feel themselves growing stronger in joy, in hope, in God.

I drain the sink, brushing away whatever's spilled down my cheeks with the back of my hand, but I am filling, my heart filling with thankfulness for grace even now, my mind filling with the hopefulness of Miriam.

No matter what hard times you see, hold on to your tambourine, give thanks, give thanks, give thanks, and trust there will be a way through waves, that you will stand on the other side— and sing with all the faith mothers this rising Song of the Sea.

ABOUT THE AUTHOR
Ann Voskamp

Photo by Levi Voskamp

Ann Voskamp is a blogger and memoirist who openly tells her brokenhearted story and seeks to find the beauty and quiet in the chaos. She has authored eight books as of 2016, including her *New York Times* bestseller *One Thousand Gifts*. She lives in Canada with her farmer husband and seven children. Find her at annvoskamp.com.

"THE PEOPLE OF *GOD* HAVE *always needed* LEADERS WHO ARE *the faith* MOTHERS."

— *Ann Voskamp*

L to R: Sandra McCracken, Sam McCracken,
Leslie Jordan, Ruth Chou Simons

HANNAH

God's Faithfulness When Life Feels Unfair

LISTEN ALONG

"Holy Place"

One of my favorite ways God shows His faithfulness is through the astounding gifts He gives. Gracious relationships with friends and family. The provision of what we need today. And even the littlest surprises—like an encouraging phone call, a perfect spring day, or an unexpected reason to belly laugh. But sometimes God's faithfulness to us becomes more obvious when He withholds things. Sometimes He allows life to feel unfair.

How do we react when life feels unfair? When we don't get the gift or desired outcome we long for? My battle plan usually goes like this: fight with everything I can muster, grow frustrated and discouraged, and finally sulk in my victimhood. Needless to say, this plan is not productive, and at the end of my own strength, I beg the Lord for a better way. In recent years, I have found help and encouragement in the story of Hannah. She teaches us how to navigate life's seemingly unfair seasons—with humble patience, deep peace, and authentic joy.

TRUE GRIT

Determination runs deep in my DNA. If I ever contemplate giving up on something or doing a half-baked job, my mom's words echo in my ears, reminding me that wimping out is never an option.

I lost my eyesight at age three due to a degenerative eye condition. So not only did I have to learn different ways of doing things, I had to learn to understand the double standard by which the world judges me and how to handle that judgment.

My earliest memories of that lesson are from when Mom first introduced me to the concepts of chores and allowance. Being paid to do work around the house? What a splendid idea! I couldn't wait to get started. My first job, when I was eight or so, was unloading the dishwasher. Mom taught me how to carefully remove each item from the top rack, line the dishes up on the counter, close the door, put them away, and then do the bottom rack. An extremely fun task, I thought! I felt so grown up and responsible. For several weeks I looked forward to dishwashers full of clean dishes. I even contributed extra so we could run it sooner.

I enjoyed this newfound chore-doing so much that next Mom taught me how to clean the bathroom. Scrubbing the tub, toilet, and sink took a bit more time than dishes, but it was still a delightful task—for a few weeks, anyway.

Soon chores began to get in the way of fun. They were "hard," I whined. Tedious. They took a precious hour of my Saturday. I expressed to Mom that I'd prefer to do chores only sometimes.

Instead of simply insisting I do the work, Mom wisely reasoned that in order for me to be independent and have my own place one day, I'd need to be able to do chores well. If people came to my house and it was messy, they wouldn't think me lazy but incapable of doing better because I couldn't see.

When I tired of ironing my clothes, she reminded me, "If you walk out of the house all wrinkled, people won't think it's because you were in a rush; they'll think you can't iron because you're blind. You don't want the 'bless her heart' treatment." ("Bless her heart" is Southern for many things, including "More cannot be expected of her. Feel sorry for her.") Mom was right. I didn't want such treatment.

I found this to be true with more real-world experiences. I remember going to cheerleading camp one summer in high school. Lots of teams were packed into one gym learning the same routines. Since I couldn't see what everyone was doing, I had to perform the dance steps from memory. I memorize things all the time, and I was usually pretty good at learning new routines. But that day I kept making mistakes. I finally burst into tears in front of the entire camp. An awkward, painful hush fell over the room. I could almost hear all the cheerleaders thinking "bless her

heart" thoughts. I knew I was just having an off day—unrelated to my sight—but they didn't. The utter irritation of this made me cry even harder. I despised the helpless feeling that came with the tears, so after they dried, I willed myself never to crack again. From then on, determination was my armor; grit was my guide.

> *"The work of earning, and then maintaining, our place in the world is a relentless, endless, exhausting pursuit."*

This inner grit got me far in life.

I learned early on that being different could lead to isolation and sadness, unless I took matters into my own hands. Making a better life was up to me. As I did my weekly chores around the house or learned new skills like putting on makeup, I knew all of it was preparing me for the future. Mastering each new task gave me confidence that

I could do almost anything I set my mind to and that my drive to do so would help me thrive in a sighted world. But there is a problem with this sort of internal force. At some point, it runs out.

The work of earning, and then maintaining, our place in the world is a relentless, endless, exhausting pursuit that eventually drains us of all our spirit. Then we falter and feel like a failure. We try to recover by gritting it out, and we fail again. After a million cycles of this, I had to face the reality that no amount of inner grit could bring me inner peace. When I got to that point, I had to learn a new set of steps to lead me down the path of true strength.

This is where Hannah comes in.

ADMITTING DEFEAT

Hannah's story and song are found at the beginning of *1 Samuel*. In her song, we hear her sing of joy and strength: *"My heart rejoices in the LORD; in the LORD my horn is lifted high" (2:1).* But this is far from the place where she began. Hannah's story opens with the revelation of her utterly miserable circumstances. She was one of two wives, which never results in peace. In fact, the other wife, Peninnah, was referred to as *"her rival" (1:6–7).* To make matters worse, Hannah could not have children.

In today's world, being unable to conceive is an incredible heartbreak for many, but being childless in Hannah's day meant a woman had no value whatsoever. Year after year, Hannah, Peninnah, and their husband, Elkanah, traveled to the tabernacle in Shiloh to worship God. And year after year, Peninnah bullied her because Hannah had no children, to the point that *"she wept and would not eat" (v. 7).* Hannah's loving—but super insensitive—husband asked her why she was crying: *"Don't I mean more to you than ten sons?" (v. 8).*

Though we don't have insight into Hannah's life beyond the tabernacle, Scripture says Elkanah loved her very much, so we can infer that she was likely his first wife. Not only is she named first, but he probably would not have taken a second wife if she had been able to conceive. We can imagine, then, that Hannah didn't spend every day grieving. I bet she often tapped into her own inner grit—going about her day-to-day, responding to her husband's love, and maintaining calm around Peninnah and her kids. Yet because she had no children of her own, she lived in a perpetual state of sadness and longing. For her, all the pain and drama came to a head every year at the time of worship. She was victimized—battling infertility, lack of empathy from her husband, and bullying from another woman.

Then came the moment at Shiloh when Hannah had enough. Broken and defeated, she chose to step away from the chaos that had kept her from worshipping the Lord for so long. She ran straight into the arms of Yahweh (God), laying before Him all the things that held them miles apart. He met her there in her brokenness. In this meeting with God, this place of emptying and receiving, Hannah found true strength.

～

For most of my life, the mental noise of navigating a sighted world kept me from trusting completely that God actually wanted to give me relentless strength. Ever since I can remember, my tendency was to rely on my own abilities instead of fully leaning on Him. Even as Mom was teaching me to take the first steps toward independence and therefore confidence, I felt the pain and loneliness of middle school bullying. As the only blind student in my public school classes, I lived in fear of making a mistake and getting ostracized for it—which was a daily occurrence. Girls I desperately wanted to be friends with made jokes about how I was the stupidest, most awkward girl in class. Everyone laughed. I desperately tried to find ways to earn their approval. But for the most part, recesses and lunchtimes were spent in isolation, while in my estimation, all the "normal" kids were having fun around me. The seemingly endless days of humiliation and rejection left me feeling weak and helpless, insignificant and alone.

After one of my darkest days of bullying, my mom insisted, "Ginny, Jesus is always your best friend, but some days it may feel like He's your only friend." She assured me I could tell Him everything, because not only did He see and know everything I was facing but He had experienced the worst bullying—the worst darkness imaginable. To cry out to Him was to cry out to a personal God who knew my struggles firsthand.

I accepted her words in theory, but I did not know how to actually tap into the fortitude He could give. Even though He was there to hear prayers and oversee things, I thought my inner strength was the key to my success.

MEETING WITH GOD

Hannah beautifully demonstrates meeting with God in vulnerability. In *1 Samuel 1*, she entered the tabernacle, and in deep brokenness with many tears, she poured out her heart to the Lord. She did not simply resign herself to her circumstances and praise God anyway. She brought her aching heart and passionately prayed about what weighed her down. In her weakness, she came and offered up her desire to the only One who could bring change:

———

Lord Almighty, if you will only look on your servant's misery and remember me, and not forget your servant but give her a son, then I will give him to the Lord for all the days of his life. (1:11)

———

As Hannah prayed, several things became immediately clear. She knew the Lord she talked to is all powerful; she called Him *"Lord of Armies" (csb)* or *"Lord of hosts" (esv)*. The One who held her life, and the world, in His capable hands heard her prayer longing for children, revealing another beautiful, powerful aspect of prayer: the God of creation cares about every detail of our lives. Along with praying for a son, Hannah gave God her anxiety and bitterness—her deepest sadness and darkness—that held her prisoner. In giving the longings in the recesses of her heart to the God who created her, no walls stood between them. We see how God's faithful empowering began in the confessing, the lamenting, and the offering of Hannah's prayer. Meeting

the Lord in prayer requires our total honesty and trust that He hears and wants to work in every heartache we lay before Him.

"*To cry out to Him was to cry out to a personal God who knew my struggles firsthand.*"

In this dark time in Israel, Eli, the priest, was not used to seeing people pour out their prayers to God. When he saw her praying, he mistakenly accused Hannah of being drunk. Hannah insisted she was sober, but she wasted no time in confessing her current state—a broken woman with a broken heart. *"I've been praying from the depth of my anguish and resentment,"* she told him *(v. 16 csb)*. Hannah honestly voiced her vulnerability to Eli, revealing there is no shame in coming to God and to those we trust, in however many pieces we're in.

Though she did not know how the Lord would answer her request,

Hannah walked away from her meeting with God a changed woman. She was finally able to eat, and her face no longer wore an expression of exhaustion and hopelessness. She laid her cares and weakness on the shoulders of the One who cares the most, and in return, God offered His power to stabilize her. She gave God her desire, and He gave her Himself. She could worship Him, regardless of what happened next.

> *"At our core, many of us believe prayer is a nice idea, but at the end of the day, we think it is up to us to save ourselves."*

At our core, many of us believe prayer is a nice idea, but at the end of the day, we think it is up to us to save ourselves. I have many friends who rely on the relentless inner grit they've developed. Their relationship with God is, at best, distant and polite. They aren't interested in meeting with Him. Their reason: day in and day out, they have battled a painful life challenge and begged Him for a change. But no answer has come. No rescue from their constant turmoil. Now they assume that if there's a God, He must not care about our daily challenges. Or perhaps He wants us to figure things out on our own. Or even worse, maybe He isn't actually good, like we were told growing up in church. We tend to find it difficult to believe in a good, listening God when our circumstances remain overwhelming. So instead of coming to Him with all our deepest resentment, anger, sadness, and desires, we trust in our own strength. We grit it out and face the world on our own.

This is certainly where I used to live. I didn't talk to God much about people's hurtful reactions to my blindness. I assumed they were a trial meant to toughen me up and, if I ever became a super Christian, I'd be able to rise above the pain. I'm thankful to be long past the bullying era of my teens, but I'm still met with fear and misunderstanding, and the accompanying feeling that I am less than often leaves me brokenhearted. At times, I have chosen to feel like a victim.

I lamented to a friend one day, "I have done everything I can to prove myself. I run my own ministry, and I've had great adventures as a musician. I think I'm generally well put together. So why can't I meet people's expectations? Why do so many see me as someone to be pitied, not an equal or a potential friend?" After thinking for a moment, I admitted perhaps the more honest question: "Why can't I meet my own expectations?"

> ## "His strength took root in me, overpowering my weak, human version."

"What do you think God thinks of your struggles?" she asked after a long pause. "How do you think He feels when He sees people being unkind or dismissive? Or when He sees the unbelievable pressure you put on yourself?"

I did not know.

As I prayed and asked God to show me, He began to reveal His heart to me. When I read about Jesus healing people with all types of challenges, inviting others out of their fear and doubt, and weeping before He raised Lazarus from the dead, I realized how He aches over our suffering and heartbreak. His longing is for me to come to Him, with honesty and vulnerability, emptying everything in the recesses of my heart. Because I hadn't taken my challenges of being blind to Him, I had held many other things back as well. Trying to manage on my own had driven a wedge between us.

As I read God's words and met Him in prayer, seeing and experiencing the beauty of His heart, His strength took root in me, overpowering my weak, human version. I began to change though my circumstances were the same. Like Hannah, my heart slowly rose above them in a chorus of courage.

STRENGTH IN WEAKNESS

In Hannah's song from 1 Samuel 2, she sang about her great God who reverses fortunes—giving children to the childless woman and filling the hungry. Her all-powerful God can bring poverty or lift up the poor, giving them *"a throne of honor" (vv. 7–8)*. But in the same song, Hannah also sang of failure for anyone who felt confident enough to trust their own strength instead of God's. Hannah learned these truths firsthand. God allowed Hannah to be childless for some time, and then He gave her—the weak, heckled, misunderstood, barren woman—a son.

After raising him for several years, Hannah willingly gave her son back to God. As she promised, she took him to the tabernacle to live with the Lord, saying, *"I prayed for this child, and the LORD has granted me what I asked of him. So now I give him to the LORD"* (1:27–28). To understand this type of action in today's terms: one of my seminary professors described it as similar to sending your child away to boarding school and only visiting him once or twice a year.

Year after year, when Hannah came to worship at the tabernacle, she brought her son new clothes she made for him. How astounding was that? Hannah returned to the place of worship with her husband and her rival—again with no child—bringing clothes to the son she gave back to God. But Hannah was now different. She sang. She worshipped. (Eli offered an annual blessing over Hannah and her husband that God would give them more children, and He eventually did.) Until then, how did Hannah sing and worship in these circumstances—separated from her only son? Quite simply, Hannah's Lord, not her longing, was now at the center of her soul.

Hannah's meeting with God brought her to a very childlike yet mature belief that God is in charge. Loving Him more than everything and everyone else gave her resilience to do even the most difficult things. In other words, Hannah's strength came from resting in God's strength. Her hope grew as she trusted Him as her salvation, her rock, and her rescuer. After meeting with Him in prayer, she believed that because He is faithful, whatever He allowed in her life would be the best and right thing. And He alone would give her joy and courage to stay the course. Several years ago, I wrote a chorus that said it this way:

> Thank You, Lord;
> You don't always give me
>   what I ask for.
> Even when I'm crying out
>   that I'm sure,
> You see what I can't see
> and give me what I need.[1]

I struggle daily to live in God's strength, because it means I have to accept being weak. Though God has allowed the outward weakness of my blindness, my inner weaknesses are much more challenging. A common weakness for a driven "entertainer" like me is worrying about how I am perceived. Yet as I revel in my identity in Christ, I know that my drive and determination alone will never be enough to sustain me, nor will the attitudes of others be enough to break me. God faithfully created me, and He gives me true freedom to be that person and release my need to control what other people think.

> "God faithfully created me, and He gives me true freedom to be that person and release my need to control what other people think."

How does that play out in real life? It means I look at how the Lord sees me—as His dearly loved daughter, the recipient of His finished work on the cross. I don't look at how I or anyone else evaluates me. As Timothy Keller says, "The essence of gospel humility is not thinking more of myself or less of myself; it is thinking of myself less."[2]

If others think I'm weak, they're right. I can't do life on my own, and I'm becoming ever more confident in that fact. Like Hannah, who found relentless fortitude as she rested in the arms of her heavenly Father, I realized at some point that my drive to appear strong not only put a wall between God and me but between myself and others. Turns out people have lots of questions about how I do life, and my lack of vulnerability had kept them from asking. I cracked open the door by creating a video series called *How I See It*, where I show how I accomplish everyday tasks like putting on makeup. When I began sharing these videos and similar experiences from my personal life, great conversations started happening. Not only did I answer curious questions, but the door swung open for others who live with life challenges to tell their stories and find freedom from gritting it out on their own.

God's generous strength means I can rest and stop trying to appear impressive, perfectly put together, or independent. It means sometimes I accept help I don't think I need because God is providing the opportunity for me to connect with someone new. It means I focus my attention on doing what the Lord has put in front of me: serving, encouraging, and helping bring change.

It means my inner grit now comes from the power of the cross.

THE BIGGER STORY

God and Hannah's meeting forever changed the course of history. Her son Samuel led Israel out of the darkest period they had yet known. The Lord's power brought him resilience as God had given his mother, and he challenged the nation of Israel to once again find its strength in God. He later anointed King David, the king after God's own heart.

Hannah's song of praise speaks of things that had not yet happened: *"He will give strength to his king and exalt the horn of his anointed" (2:10b).* She sang of the anointed one to come, not knowing that Israel would soon be led by kings instead of judges. That, a thousand years later, another joyful song of strength would be sung by a young woman soon to deliver God's ultimate anointed King:

———

He has done a mighty deed with
his arm;
he has scattered the proud
because of the thoughts of their hearts;...
He has helped his servant Israel,
remembering his mercy
to Abraham and his descendants
forever. (Luke 1:51, 54–55 CSB)

———

Both Hannah and Mary sang of how weak and powerless humans are, compared to how strong and powerful God is. What's more, they sang of how He loves and remembers His people. In His love, God chose to become a weak and humble human being so we could gain strength that lasts forever. *"He was oppressed and afflicted, yet he did not open his mouth" (Isa. 53:7 CSB).* The more we are moved by Jesus' choice to show Himself weak on our behalf, the more wholeheartedly we can sing of and rest in the strength He gives.[3]

*L to R: Trillia Newbell,
Ginny Owens, Christy Nockels*

Lord, thank You that You not only see but allow every circumstance I face. Thank You that I can come before You in my weakness and uncertainty and receive Your strength. Help me bring all my questions, longings, and tears to You, knowing that even if You don't bring immediate change, You are working all things together for Your glory and my good. Remind me that You chose to be weak so that I could gain eternal strength. In light of this, teach me to be like Hannah, laying down my victim mentality in favor of worshipping You.

Amen.

ABOUT THE AUTHOR
Ginny Owens

Photo by Jessica Grande

An award-winning musician, author, and speaker, Ginny Owens was born and raised in Jackson, Mississippi, and discovered melodies on the piano before she could complete a sentence. When a degenerative eye condition left Ginny completely blind by age three, songs provided a window into the world. Her unique musical style and inspirational lyrics have afforded her audiences at the White House, the Sundance Film Festival, and the National Day of Prayer in Washington, DC. She has composed for artists including Michael Card, Michael W. Smith, JJ Heller, and Rachael Lampa and was named Gospel Music Association's New Artist of the Year in 2000. Her recent book is *Singing in the Dark*. Find more information, including Ginny's blog, at ginnyowens.com.

"MEETING *the Lord* IN *PRAYER* REQUIRES OUR TOTAL *honesty* AND *TRUST* THAT *He hears* AND WANTS TO WORK IN *EVERY* HEARTACHE *we* LAY *BEFORE* HIM."

— *Ginny Owens*

Front L to R: Leslie Jordan, Ginny Owens, Sally Lloyd-Jones,
Ruth Chou Simons, Ellie Holcomb, Raechel Myers, Trillia Newbell
Back L to R: Christy Nockels, Amy Grant, Sarah Macintosh,
Lisa Harper, Kelly Minter, Amanda Bible Williams

Reflections

BY SARAH MACINTOSH

I'll admit it—I was shocked when I was first asked to be a part of this project. But the shock didn't linger; it turned quickly into delight. Although the role I was asked to serve in the project is uncommon and even difficult to describe, I know it well. I have also seen, heard, and felt its life-giving effects so many times that I was able to walk my unfamous, unknown, and non-degree-holding self confidently into a room with some of the most gifted treasures that writing has to offer and lead them in writing. Just a sampling:

- Revolutionary biblical translator? *Check!*

- Unbelievably humble yet iconic musician? *Check!*
- *New York Times* bestselling author, eh? *Check!*
- Americana songbird whose voice raises hands, hearts, and arm hair? *Check!*

The role I am describing is one of a writing workshop leader for a nonprofit called the Fold. The organization, birthed and nurtured in 2016 by my dear friend and fellow musician/songwriter Leslie Jordan, has fervently sought to serve writers in a way that is greatly needed yet often overlooked. The Fold's vision is "helping writers and songwriters find their original voice in the safety of community"[1]—and oh, how it has, not only for others, but also for me.

I was born and raised in Texas. I am fluent in drawl and y'all language. Still to this day, though I no longer live in Texas, when I hear someone speaking from my place of origin, I can feel my shoulders relax and my heart rate slow.

After moving from Texas in the middle of my senior year of high school, I arrived in frosty Boulder, Colorado, where my beloved Texas tongue was hated, berated, and demeaned. I understood why my voice was met with such dislike by those in Boulder: Texans and Californians were flooding into that beautiful state, driving up home prices, crowding freeways and ski resorts, and bringing with them the immaturity and lack of respect that often come with a tourist or out-of-towner mindset. They were also filling the sky with smog faster than nature could disperse it.

As a result, my ideas and personhood were judged based on whether I introduced myself as Sarah or, as my Deedee called me, Say-ruh. I am embarrassed to say that I abandoned my accent. I wanted to belong, to be heard, to be understood and known for who I was, not who my Texas accent led others to believe I was. Without truly realizing it, I covered my voice over, flattened it out, and stamped down upon any bit of character left in the way I said my words, till my language sounded like the native tongue of nowhere.

Although I sometimes feel saddened by the loss of my drawl, nothing compares to the sadness I feel when I think about the years I spent silencing my original voice. When there is shame saying "Say-ruh," there is shame being Say-ruh.

In the years that followed, I traveled as a singer, speaker, and songwriter, all the while continuing to allow others to rename me again and again. Each time, I adjusted my voice to conform to their preferences. I bent my God-created being, believing I would receive the belonging, acceptance, and knowing that I craved. My desire was for them, and they ruled over me.

It took years before I could see how spiritually emaciated I had become, yet through God's intimate and intentional persistence—God's faithfulness—I finally saw. The revelation came while I was in community with others who were spiritually emaciated as well. Others who shared the native tongue of nowhere in order to belong somewhere. Others who had given up their original voice. Our need, our starved state, hummed along with David's as he sang:

———

When I kept silent, my bones wasted away through my groaning all day long. For day and night your hand was heavy on me; my strength was sapped as in the heat of summer. (Ps. 32:3–4)

———

And in that shared song, we found the belonging we had been seeking. Yes, within the Fold, through the safety curated by Leslie Jordan, the silence of our original voices was broken.

Pat Schneider, who taught writing, says in her book *How the Light Gets In,*

> In my own original voice lies the foundation, the authority, the orientation, the perspective I need in order to use other voices.... That first voice, the voice of home, is the one the writer must protect from the contempt or disdain or disregard of any critic, no matter how famous or capable that critic may be. It is not all that a mature writer needs ... but a profound acceptance of and trust in one's own voice is the first and most important thing the writer needs.[1]

In spring, summer, fall, and winter, writers arrive into the Fold, sometimes laughing, sometimes limping. At the workshops and retreats, shoulders relax, heart rates slow, and the writers speak again in their original voice. It slips off their tongues like the delicacy it is, and we listen. As a result, our world grows larger and God becomes clearer and more understandable, humanity more beautiful, and life more abundant.

In those moments, the scarcity that comes with silence is over, and we feast on the sound of their God-given voices. Within the Fold, writers have the safety and nurturing to go back to the beginning, to speak with their original voice, born again.

"Sit with the knowledge that when you write, you will always be met with freedom and encouragement."

It was for this purpose that I was asked to join the Faithful project. During three writing retreats, I sat with the authors and songwriters of Faithful, leading them in writing sessions to call to their original voices.

The dreamers and nurturers of the project hoped to create an environment in the retreats where the writers would find inspiration, companionship, and freedom in community with each other—and, oh, how they did. Oh, how they laughed, cried, clapped, oohed, and aahed over even the little bits of writing that came from prompts as simple as "Randomly grab a record from a shelf, and with a seven-minute time limit, say anything and everything."

I have tears again now as I remember the treasured words that were laid fearfully and humbly at our feet and the responses of the listening women affirming the strengths, wonderful surprises, and unforgettable moments in their written pieces. Yes, we delighted in the voices of one another, and the feeling has remained like warmth in our chests.

Is it any wonder that we would like to share this experience with you? No, because like the "we" speaking in *1 John 1:4*, we also desire *"that your joy may be full" (KJV)*. Yes, that would complete our joy. So share in this experience with us.

First, begin as we did, knowing that a writer is simply someone who writes. Sit with the knowledge that when you write, you will always be met with freedom and encouragement. There is no incorrect way to follow these prompts. You can write a list, story, text, poem, journal entry, or song. Each, any, or all will be fruitful.

Second, prepare a space for yourself and your writing. This can mean anything from setting aside time and a location to starting the practice of carrying around a piece of paper and small pencil in your pocket for when inspiration strikes.

Third, write from the same spirit found in *1 John 1:1–4*, which we ourselves read and returned to throughout the retreats. Hold it with you as well while you write. Let the prompts aid you in this. In the words of Eugene Peterson's *The Message*, the verses read:

———

From the very first day, we were there, taking it all in—we heard it with our own ears, saw it with our own eyes, verified it with our own hands. The Word of Life appeared right before our eyes; we saw it happen! And now we're telling you in most sober prose that what we witnessed was, incredibly, this: The infinite Life of God himself took shape before us.

We saw it, we heard it, and now we're telling you so you can experience it along with us, this experience of communion with the Father and his Son, Jesus Christ. Our motive for writing is simply this: We want you to enjoy this, too. Your joy will double our joy!

———

So, *Faithful* reader, we invite you to join us with your own voice. Write about what you have heard with your own ears, seen with your own eyes, and felt with your own hands. Yes, speak.

01 | We Have Heard

READ/LISTEN TO *"The Detour."*

Spend fifteen minutes writing, using the prompt

"I have heard..."

This time will not be wasted
All the sorrow I have tasted
You sing Hope across the valley of my tears
Sometimes love looks like delay
But You walk me through the wait
and I am learning laughter even here
You are with me here

READ/LISTEN TO *"God Above, God Below (Rachel's Lullaby)."*

Spend ten minutes writing, using the prompt

"I hear..."

I will tell you like it is:
I was hanging by a thread
Pushed out to the furthest edge
        and I wasn't proud of it
From my home within the wall
Always face to face with dark
Oh, I wondered if I knew the light at all

I was sure my heart would melt from fear
But there was One who held me even there

He is God above, He is God below
He is God of everything between
There's no place you'll be where He cannot go
Look at my face, these eyes have seen
I know the Lord

*Grab a pen and a journal. What have you seen? What
have you heard? What have you felt?*

01

READ/LISTEN TO *"Rise Up."*

**Spend seven minutes writing,
using the prompt**

"I want to hear…"

> Tell me the story of the girl without a mother
> Of the girl without a father
> Who found favor with the king
> Tell me again about how he beheld her beauty,
> About the way she stepped out bravely
> All her life an offering
>
> She fell to her knees, while she begged him "Please
> Spare my people. Oh, set them free, oh king!"
>
> "Give them unmerited belonging to a kingdom that is coming
> It's the song that they'll keep on singin',
>   It's the bells they'll keep on ringin'
> I'm swept into a story, oh, that I don't want to miss
> So I will rise up for such a time as this."

02 | *We Have Seen*

READ/LISTEN TO *"Impossible Things."*

Spend fifteen minutes writing, using
the prompt

"I have seen..."

> I know, I know I've been here before
>   facedown on the floor
> Same dance, same song through my sighs and groans
>   barely holding on
>
> You were enough for me then, You'll be enough for me now
> And that's enough to hope a little longer.
>
> For impossible things, You do impossible things
> You open my eyes, that I will survive this impossible thing

Grab a pen and a journal. What have you seen? What have you heard? What have you felt?

02

READ/LISTEN TO *"Holy Place."*

Spend ten minutes writing, using the prompt

"I see..."

And when we look to You
When we seek Your face
Any simple room is a holy place
So lead us by the hand,
       teach our longing hearts
That all we've ever needed
       is to be where You are

READ/LISTEN TO *"At This Very Time."*

Spend seven minutes writing, using the prompt

"I want to see..."

We walk in assurance of what we can't see
We long for the city that is yet to be
Our God is a shelter, our help and our stay
We rest in His arms and His unchanging grace

03 | *We Have Felt*

READ/LISTEN TO *"You Came for Me."*

Spend fifteen minutes writing, using the prompt

"I have felt..."

Hiding in plain sight,
      praying for some peace
Carrying my burden,
      looking for relief
Wearied as I was,
      I felt You close to me
Reaching out Your hand,
      You offered me a drink

You came for me

READ/LISTEN TO *"We Are One."*

Spend ten minutes writing, using the prompt

"I feel..."

Travelers, misfits, and exiles
Don't grow cold in the dark of the night
Gather for hope and for comfort
In His light, His light

Let us draw near to each other
We are one, we are one
We are all sisters and brothers
Warming hands by the fire of His love

Grab a pen and a journal. What have you seen? What have you heard? What have you felt?

03

READ/LISTEN TO *"We Do Not Labor in Vain."*

Spend seven minutes writing, using the prompt

"I want to feel..."

This is the groaning
        as You count every tear we have sown
And we trust what those tears will become
This is the stretching
        making room for our hope to arrive
Knowing You come to make us alive
To make us alive

We wait for light, we wait for rain
Behold the life born out of pain
Eyes to the dawn, we're not afraid
We do not labor in vain

04 | *We Will Speak*

READ/LISTEN TO *"Call upon Him."*

Spend fifteen minutes writing, using
the prompt

"I have said..."

> When I don't have the words
> When the spirit hurts
> When my sorrow's too deep to
> understand
> Will You hear my voice saying
> "Speak, oh Lord
> Mighty God, Healing King,
> take my hand"?
>
> Call upon Him, call upon Him
> There is power in the name

Grab a pen and a journal. What have you seen? What have you heard? What have you felt?

04

READ/LISTEN TO

"This Time I Will Bring Praise."

Spend ten minutes writing, using the prompt

"I say…"

I have been unchosen, hidden, and unseen
Fighting disappointment with insufficient
    strength,
You have seen it all, and You say I belong

So I lift my eyes up to the heavens
You're my help, Lord, I surrender

This time, this time, I will bring praise
I will bring praise to the Lord
This time, this time, I will give thanks
I will give thanks to the Lord

READ/LISTEN TO *"A Woman."*

Spend seven minutes writing, using the prompt

"I will say…"

So I will run and tell the story
Oh, the Word did not stay buried
but it is alive!
Spirit setting tongues on fire!

Listen, the heavens singing
       "Glory, glory, glory!"
Trees are clapping, clapping, clapping!
Rocks are shouting, shouting, shouting!

And then there's me, a woman

And I will speak …

Believing im alone
not a lie

too far   - IM
not enough   - 14
too late   - sta
too small
afraid
its too dark

ABOUT THE AUTHOR
Sarah MacIntosh

Sarah MacIntosh is a mother of many things, first to two amazing human beings. In her spare time, she also mothers words, thoughts, and creators. In this role, she cherishes, protects, and cares for them in their living, moving, and breathing. She brings a similar admiration and carefulness to her time with the Word. Sarah and her two children live on a few acres of land in Franklin, Tennessee, narrowly warding off ticks while on the hunt for wonder.

The Story
Of Faithful

We are beyond thrilled that you're holding this book in your hands. Years of work, prayer, and community have poured into the pages you've been reading.

At its heart, this project is the fruit of many friendships. Keely, David, and Andrew go back twenty years, and Susan was a more recent—and most welcome—addition. And then there are the friendships of the women who gathered, both old and new.

Faithful began as independent dreams. Among us there were ideas of a collaborative community project by women, of pairing songwriters and authors to create together, and of a project focusing on putting flesh and blood on the women characters in the Bible.

We started to wonder what might result from bringing together experienced artists with up-and-coming musicians ... bringing together Christian women who were writers, Bible scholars, songwriters, and musicians in writing camps ... to create an album, a book (the one you're reading right now), or an event, all founded on the concept of God's faithfulness to women.

As we continued to naturally share our ideas over coffee or when our work on other projects intersected, we realized we were in an incredibly fruitful place: we had dreams that overlapped, and we were part of organizations with the resources (and shared mission) to make those dreams actually happen. How could we not attempt to pull this off!?

We began by inviting friends from our author and songwriter worlds to gather at the historic Art House. This old Nashville church was converted into an iconic recording studio and has become a revered home for the discussion of arts and faith. There we shared our vision and invited other friends to join us.

To be honest, it got a little scary there for a minute as we revealed our dreams of what this project could be. We didn't want to ask too much, so we shared only about half of what we envisioned. These women graciously took our idea, disassembled it, pushed on it here and pulled on it there, and then reassembled it as the exact thing we had hoped for but didn't think would be possible. This time, however, it was not just our little team's idea but it belonged to a whole community.

From there the momentum began to build. We invited our friends back to the Art House for two days of group writing exercises (led by our fearless guide, Sarah Macintosh), songwriting, and precious time together. Our dinner table overflowed with rich conversation and deep laughter.

In the mornings, our authors and songwriters broke off into songwriting groups, where they were each given the name of a different woman in the Bible as a starting point for their creative time together.

It was the most incredible sound to walk the hallway of the studio and overhear these beautiful melodies, the buzzing sounds of intense discussion, and the laughter and tears ringing through the air as women dove into their ancient sisters' stories, only to find themselves sharing their own with each other.

In the evenings, we sat back in the living room of the Art House and, one by one, our friends shared with us the stories and songs they'd written. We were completely overwhelmed by the passion, insight, and stunning creativity of the beauty washing over us.

We realized then that authors always write alone and that while songwriters in Nashville often write in groups, they are rarely groups of women—and almost never is a Bible scholar in the mix! We experienced on those nights a kind of song we'd never heard before. Stories that had been hidden in the dark were walking out, nervous but hopeful, into a room bathed in candlelight and friendship.

And the fruit of this time together was profound:

Each song heard on *Faithful*, the album, was played for the first time on those incredible evenings.

Each chapter of this book was drawn directly from the conversation its author had in the songwriting rooms.

Faithful, the tour, gets to share these sweet and sacred evenings with communities all across America.

Each of these unique expressions (the album, book, and tour) lets us swing wide the door and invite you to join us in that living room, to experience with us the creativity, honesty, and friendship that can be found in the shelter of God's faithfulness.

In the end, what we know is this: Jesus rose from the dead and appeared first to Mary Magdalene. He looked at her, His dear friend, and she looked at Him. Then He asked her, a woman, to go and speak of what she had seen.

We don't believe that Jesus has stopped asking women, His friends, to speak of what they have seen.

We are incredibly thankful for our author and songwriter friends who have joined us in the telling. This entire project might have been just a chat over coffee that went nowhere without their joyful willingness to be part of this with us.

We have each been deeply impacted by what this Faithful community has created. What a joy it is, like a farmer at their table at the end of the day, to be fed by what the Lord has made from the works of our hands.

It is our deep prayer that what the Lord has made of it will, in His own time and way, feed you too.

The Faithful Team

Keely Scott (Compassion International)
Susan McPherson (David C Cook Publishing)
Andrew Osenga (Integrity Music)
David McCollum (Halogen Entertainment)

Painting created by Ruth Chou
Simons during Faithful writing camp

L to R: Tamar Chipp, Trillia Newbell

Kelly Needham

Tamar Chipp

Rachael Lampa

L to R: Christa Wells, Sarah Kroger

L to R: Taylor Leonhardt, Janice Gaines, Trillia Newbell

Acknowledgments

The team behind Faithful would like to extend our heartfelt gratitude to the many people who have contributed to the heart and soul of this project.

Nate and Cassie Tasker and family, hosts of the writing workshops at the Art House Nashville; Nathan Nockels, album producer; Sarah Macintosh, retreat workshop leader from the Fold and album coproducer; Leslie Jordan, executive director and cofounder of the Fold.

The Design team: Morgan Brewer and the team at Studio Antheia; Jordan Rubino, design coordinator, Integrity Music; Natalie Simmons, videographer; Caroline Sims, videographer; Joy Prouty, photographer.

David McCollum, Michael Blanton, Grace Kornegay, and Molly Tarr of Halogen Entertainment.

The David C Cook team: Susan McPherson, Stephanie Bennett, Judy Gillispie, Jeff Gerke, Susan Murdock, Michael Covington, Amy Konyndyk, Annette Brickbealer, Michele Baird, Elizabeth Phelps, and Kyle Berg.

The Compassion International team: Keely Scott, Steve Jones, Spence Smith, Jason Jamison, Kandee Cheek, Lynette Van Eaton, Jessica Futrell, Zane King, Walt Smith, Karen Bobo, Demetrus Alexander, Brian Seay, Tamara Moore, Jordan Smith, Beverley Bashor, Tamara Moore, Jordan Smith, and Annette Ceniceros.

The Integrity Music team: Andrew Osenga, Jonathan Brown, Adrian Thompson, Mark Nicholas, Jana Zachman, Nicole Koester, Morgan Shirey, Sarah Chandler, Mack Taylor, Katy Lively, Karen Davis, Raegan Harris, Cara Cunningham, Malcolm DuPlessis, Jonathan Lane, Greg Bays, Alaina Pol, and Gilbert Nanlohy.

As we reflect on the course of this undertaking, this project does not exist without the early vision, support, encouragement, and refinement dealt by so many. Though we could not thank each person individually, we are so grateful for their kindness and generosity of spirit.

Notes

CHAPTER 2: RUTH

1. Daniel I. Block, quoted in Robert L. Hubbard Jr., *The Book of Ruth*, The New International Commentary on the Old Testament (Grand Rapids: Eerdmans, 1988), 104.

CHAPTER 6: EVE

1. There is more to the story which we have not included here in the interest of space, but you can read the full story in Genesis 3.
2. Proverbs 8:30–31. Common English Bible © 2012. All rights reserved.
3. Ezekiel 36:9 KJV "For, behold, I am for you."
4. Matthew 1:22–23.
5. Derek Kidner, *Genesis: An Introduction and Commentary*, Kidner Classic Commentaries (Downers Grove, IL: IVP Academic, 1967), 71.
6. "The *protoevangelium*—the first glimmer of the gospel," from Kidner, *Genesis*, 70.
7. This idea I first heard in a talk by D. A. Carson quoting Kidner, *Genesis*, 68.

CHAPTER 8: NAOMI

1. Adapted from Trillia Newbell, "Dark Clouds and Abundant Grace," in *Soul Bare*, ed. Cara Sexton (Downers Grove, IL: IVP Books, 2016), 21–24.

CHAPTER 9: ESTHER

1. Ahasuerus is the Hebrew rendering of Xerxes.
2. Michael Card, *Inexpressible: Hesed and the Mystery of God's Lovingkindness* (Downers Grove, IL: IVP Books, 2018), 5.
3. Aristotle, *Poetics* 1.6.

CHAPTER 10: MIRIAM

1. Darby Translation by John Nelson Darby (1890), public domain, www.biblegateway.com/versions/Darby-Translation-Bible/.
2. Name passed down in Jewish tradition, https://jwa.org/encyclopedia /article/daughter-of-pharaoh-midrash-and-aggadah.
3. Talmud, Taanit 9a; Targum Micha 6:4, quoted in "Miriam," New World Encyclopedia, accessed June 16, 2020, www.newworldencyclopedia.org/entry/ Miriam.

CHAPTER 11: HANNAH

1. Ginny Owens, vocalist, "Thank You," by Ginny Owens and Andrew Gullahorn, track 5 on *Expressions II: Wonder*, ChickPower Music, 2021.
2. Timothy J. Keller, *The Freedom of Self-Forgetfulness*, (Chorley, UK: 10Publishing, 2012), 32.
3. Some material adapted from Ginny Owens, "A Song of Strength," in *Singing in the Dark* (Colorado Springs, CO: David C Cook, 2021).

REFLECTIONS

1. The Fold, accessed September 21, 2020, www.thefold.us.

FAITHFUL

FAITHFUL EVENTS

Gather with us for an evening of songs, stories, and friendship with the women of Faithful.

Visit **faithfulproject.com** for more info.

FAITHFUL

GO AND SPEAK

FEATURING THE SONGS:

A Woman

At This Very Time

Call Upon Him

The Detour

God Above, God Below (Rahab's Lullaby)

Holy Place

Impossible Things

Rise Up

This Time I Will Bring Praise

We Do Not Labor In Vain

We Are One

You Came For Me

COMPANION ALBUM AVAILABLE NOW

FAITHFUL PODCAST

Grab a seat and join us for more conversations and stories on the *Faithful* podcast. Available everywhere.

"If anything can end poverty's lies, it's Christ's love through His church. Our sponsored children have a church community who is investing in them, teaching them about God's love for them, His plans for their life. Working to free a little child from all kinds of poverty. And these children have a sponsor—our family—who loves them dearly and tells them so every time we write."

–Ann Voskamp

Join the Faithful community and release a child from poverty in Jesus' name.

Visit **www.compassion.com/faithful** to sponsor a child.

Releasing children from poverty
Compassion®
in Jesus' name